Rabbits

The Ultimate Care Gui

www.TarversGuides.com

ISBN: 9798394774720

CONTENTS

Keeping Rabbits: A Hopping Good Time

Imagine having a friend who's as playful as a puppy, as gentle as a kitten, and as sneaky as a squirrel. Well, get ready for an incredible adventure into the world of rabbit care! Let's hop right in!

Did you know that rabbits have their own special language? Just like people, they talk to each other using behaviours, sounds, and body language! By learning their secret codes, you can become a "Bunny Buddy" and understand their deepest desires.

Taking care of a rabbit brings incredible benefits to both you and your furry friend. It can make you feel less stressed, help you understand others better, and boost your confidence. Caring for a rabbit is not just about helping them—it's about creating a loving world where both of you can thrive!

So, whether you're a curious animal lover, a compassionate soul ready to make a difference, or an adventurous spirit seeking new bunny buddies, this book is the perfect guide for you. Get ready for a thrilling journey where the bonds you create and the love you give will forever change the lives of these extraordinary creatures.

Rabbits are not only cute and cuddly, but they are also very smart and social animals. They have a language of their own, and they'll use it to communicate with you! From happy binky dances to grumpy thumps, you'll quickly become an expert in understanding their feelings and emotions.

One of the most important things to remember when keeping rabbits is that they are not like other pets. They have their own unique needs and requirements, so it's essential to do your research before bringing a bunny into your life. This book will guide you every hop of the way, ensuring both you and your rabbit have a happy and healthy life together.

Ideally, your bunny should have an indoor space where they can feel safe and comfortable. Rabbits are sensitive creatures, and they can get scared or stressed by loud noises, extreme temperatures, and predators. By providing a cozy indoor home, you'll keep your rabbit protected and happy.

Your rabbit will need a spacious enclosure or pen where they can hop, stretch, and play. Make sure it's large enough for your rabbit to stand up on their hind legs and take a few hops in any direction. Fill their home with soft bedding, hiding spots, and toys to keep them entertained and cozy.

Rabbits are known for their boundless energy and love for exploration. To keep your bunny happy and healthy, provide them with plenty of opportunities for exercise and playtime. Set up a rabbit-proof area in your home where they can roam and explore, or consider creating a secure outdoor playpen for supervised fresh air and sunshine.

One of the most exciting parts of keeping rabbits is watching them munch on their favourite foods! Rabbits have delicate digestive systems, so it's important to provide them with a balanced and nutritious diet. The main part of their diet should be hay, which keeps their teeth healthy and their tummies full. You'll also need to offer fresh vegetables, a small amount of

pellets, and the occasional treat. Just imagine the joy on your bunny's face when they discover a tasty new veggie!

Did you know that rabbits are very clean animals? They groom themselves regularly, and they even have a special built-in comb - their tongue! However, you'll still need to lend a helping hand now and then to keep your bunny's fur soft and clean.

Regularly brush your rabbit, especially if they have long hair, to prevent matting and hairballs. You'll also need to keep their living space tidy, which means cleaning their enclosure and replacing their bedding.

Just like people, rabbits need friends too! Rabbits are social creatures and thrive when they have a companion to share their life with. Having two or more rabbits can help keep them happy and prevent loneliness when you're not around. But remember, rabbits can be territorial, so make sure you introduce new friends slowly and carefully to ensure they get along.

One of the most important aspects of rabbit keeping is ensuring your furry friend stays healthy. This means regular visits to a rabbit-savvy veterinarian for check-ups, vaccinations, and any necessary treatments. Keep an eye on your rabbit's behaviour, appetite, and appearance, as any changes could indicate a health issue.

Now, you might be wondering, "How do I bond with my rabbit and become the best of friends?" The key is patience and understanding. Rabbits can be shy and cautious at first, so give them time to get to know you. Offer gentle pets, speak softly, and reward them with their favourite treats. In time, your rabbit will learn to trust you, and you'll share a special bond that lasts a lifetime.

As you continue your journey through this book, you'll discover even more tips and tricks for keeping your rabbit happy and healthy. From fun toys and games to understanding their unique behaviours, you'll become a rabbit keeping expert in no time!

So, are you ready to hop into the enchanting world of rabbit keeping? With love and patience you and your new fluffy friend will embark on a fantastic adventure filled with laughter, snuggles, and nose boops. Let the bunny-filled fun begin!

Chapter 1 - The Different Breeds of Rabbits

Did you know, there are over 300 different breeds of rabbits, each with its own unique look and personality. In this chapter, we will explore some of these enchanting breeds, so get ready to hop into the wonderful world of rabbits!

Flemish Giant Rabbit

Flemish Giant Rabbit

Let's start our journey with the Flemish Giant Rabbit. This massive breed can weigh up to 20 pounds, making them the largest of all rabbit breeds! Flemish Giants are known for their calm and friendly nature, earning them the nickname "gentle giants." They are incredibly patient and tolerant, making them fantastic pets for families with young children. Just make sure you have enough room for these big bunnies to stretch their long legs!

Holland Lop

This small, floppy-eared bunny will melt your heart with its sweet face and gentle nature. Holland Lops come in a wide variety of colours, from white to chocolate brown, and even a mix of colours called "broken." Their silky soft fur is perfect for snuggling, and their loving personalities make them wonderful pets for children and adults alike.

English Angora rabbit

With its luxurious, cloud-like fur, this breed is like a living, breathing work of art. English Angoras are known for their friendly and curious personalities, always eager to explore and learn new things. Their fur is perfect for spinning into yarn, making them a favourite among fibre artists around the world.

Rex Rabbit

Known for their velvety, plush fur and striking appearance, Rex rabbits are truly one-of-a-kind. They come in a variety of colours, from snow-white to midnight black, and even a rare blue hue. These rabbits are not only beautiful but also incredibly intelligent, making them excellent pets for those who enjoy teaching tricks and playing games with their furry friends.

Netherland Dwarf Rabbit

These miniature bunnies are like a sprinkle of happiness with their cute, round faces and short, perky ears. Netherland Dwarfs are the smallest of all rabbit breeds, making them perfect for those who have limited space or just can't resist their pint-sized charm. Despite their small size, these little bunnies have big personalities and can be quite the entertainers!

Harlequin rabbit

Netherland Dwarf Rabbit

With their striking, colourful coat patterns, these bunnies are like living, breathing pieces of art! Harlequins come in two main varieties: the Japanese Harlequin, with bold, orange and black or blue markings, and the Magpie Harlequin, with white and black or blue markings. These bunnies are not only gorgeous but also friendly and outgoing, making them excellent pets for those who appreciate both beauty and personality.

6

Mini Lop Rabbit

These medium-sized bunnies are the perfect combination of cute and cuddly, with their floppy ears and soft, plush fur. Mini Lops come in a wide range of colours and patterns, making them a popular choice for pet owners. Their easy going nature and love for attention make them fantastic companions for both children and adults.

Lionhead Rabbit

With their fluffy mane of fur around their head and neck, they look like tiny, hopping lions!

Lionhead Rabbit

Lionheads are a relatively new breed and have quickly become popular due to their striking appearance and friendly personalities. These little bundles of fluff are full of energy and love to play, making them a delightful addition to any home.

With their stunning, silver-tipped fur and bright, expressive eyes, these bunnies are truly a sight to behold. Silver Fox rabbits are known for their friendly and gentle nature, making them excellent pets for those who are lucky enough to find one. Their rare and exotic beauty, combined with their sweet personalities, make them a prized addition to any rabbit-loving home.

So there you have it, a journey through the enchanting world of rabbit breeds. From the tiny Netherland Dwarf to the massive Flemish Giant, each breed has its own unique charm and personality, making rabbits truly amazing creatures. As you explore the world of bunnies, you'll find that there's a perfect rabbit for everyone, just waiting to hop into your heart!

Chapter 2 - Rabbit Behaviour & Communication

Hop, hop, hooray! You're about to dive into the fascinating world of rabbit behaviour and communication. Rabbits are intelligent and sensitive creatures with a rich and complex way of expressing themselves. The more you learn about their behaviour, the better you'll be able to care for your fluffy friend and build a strong bond of love and trust.

Rabbits are experts at using their body language, sounds, and even their cute little noses to communicate with each other and with us, their human friends. In this chapter, we'll explore some of the most common rabbit behaviours and signals, so you can become a true bunny whisperer!

The Language of Ears

Did you know rabbits have their own language? And their ears are one of the most important tools they use to "speak" it! Paying close attention to your rabbit's ears can help you understand their emotions and needs.

1. Happy and relaxed: When a rabbit is feeling happy and comfortable, their ears will usually be standing up straight, but not stiff. They may even wiggle them a little bit!

2. Curious: If your rabbit is curious or interested in something, they might tilt their ears forward, almost like they're trying to listen more closely.

3. Scared or nervous: When rabbits are scared or feeling threatened, they will often flatten their ears against their

head. This is their way of saying, "I don't like this! Please help me feel safe."

4. Angry or aggressive: If a rabbit is feeling angry or aggressive, they might raise their ears very high and stiff, with the openings facing forward.

Sense of Smell

Rabbits have an amazing sense of smell, and they use their adorable little noses to communicate too! Have you ever noticed your rabbit twitching their nose? They do this for several reasons:

1. Sniffing the air: Rabbits twitch their nose to smell the air and gather information about their surroundings. They can pick up on scents we humans can't even detect!

2. Excitement or stress: If your rabbit is feeling excited, stressed, or scared, they might twitch their nose more quickly than usual.

3. Relaxed: When your rabbit is feeling calm and relaxed, their nose twitching might slow down or even stop for a little while.

The Art of Thumping

One of the most well-known rabbit behaviours is thumping. When a rabbit thumps their hind leg on the ground, it's like they're sounding an alarm! They do this to warn other rabbits (and you) of potential danger or to show that they're upset or scared.

If your rabbit starts thumping, try to figure out what might be causing them distress, and fix the situation if you can. Sometimes, it might just be a loud noise or an unfamiliar person that's making them feel uneasy.

Rabbits have some truly delightful ways of showing they're happy and content.

1. Binkies: A binky is a joyful jump your rabbit might do when they're feeling extra happy. They'll leap into the air and twist their body in a playful way, often kicking their legs out. It's a bunny's way of saying, "I'm so happy, I can't contain myself!"

2. Zoomies: Have you ever seen your rabbit suddenly start running around their space at top speed, changing direction quickly, and maybe even doing a few binkies along the way? That's called zoomies! It's a sign that your rabbit is feeling energetic and happy.

3. Flops: When a rabbit is feeling super relaxed and comfortable, they might suddenly flop onto their side. It might look dramatic, but don't worry – it's a sign that your rabbit trusts you and their environment enough to let their guard down.

While rabbits are generally quiet animals, they do have a few sounds they use to communicate.

1. Chattering: You might hear your rabbit softly grinding their teeth together when they're happy and content – usually during a nice petting session. This is called chattering or tooth purring.

2. Grunting: If your rabbit is feeling annoyed or threatened, they might make a low grunting sound. This is their way of saying, "Back off!"

3. Squealing or screaming: This is a sound no rabbit owner wants to hear. If your rabbit squeals or screams, it means they're in extreme pain or fear. If you hear this sound, it's important to check on your rabbit and seek veterinary help if needed.

Understanding Your Rabbit's Boundaries

Just like humans, rabbits have boundaries and personal space that they want to be respected. They might nip or growl if they feel threatened or cornered. Always approach your rabbit gently, and give them the option to move away if they want to. Never force them to interact with you, as this can damage the trust between you and your bunny friend.

Building a Bond of Trust and Love

The key to understanding your rabbit's behaviour and communication is to spend quality time with them, observe their actions, and respond to their needs with love and patience. As you grow closer to your rabbit and learn their unique "language," you'll be able to provide them with the best care possible and enjoy a deep and meaningful friendship that will last a lifetime.

In the next chapter, we'll explore how to create the perfect, cozy home for your rabbit, complete with all the essentials to keep them happy, healthy, and hopping with joy!

There are so many bunnies to choose from, each with their own unique qualities, that it can make the decision quite a challenge! That's why, dear reader, I'm here to share with you the secrets to finding the perfect rabbit for your family. So hop along with me on this exciting adventure!

Rabbits are not just adorable and cuddly creatures; they're also intelligent and social animals that can become a fantastic addition to any family. When you bring home a bunny, you're not just getting a pet - you're gaining a new family member!

Now, hold on to your bunny ears, because we're about to hop into the first step of choosing the right rabbit for your family.

Step 1: The Bunny Personality Test

Just like humans, rabbits come in all sorts of personalities. Some bunnies are shy and quiet, while others are playful and outgoing. To find the perfect rabbit for your family, you'll need to think about the kind of bunny personality that will fit in best with your home.

Are you looking for a curious adventurer who loves to explore? Or would you prefer a snuggly bunny who enjoys cuddling up and watching movies with you? Spend some time interacting with different rabbits to get a feel for their personalities. You'll soon find that each rabbit has its own unique charm that's sure to make you fall in love!

Step 2: Size and Space

Rabbits come in all shapes and sizes, from tiny little Netherland Dwarfs to the majestic Flemish Giants. Before you bring a bunny home, consider the size of the rabbit and the space you have available in your home.

Larger rabbits need more room to roam and play, while smaller bunnies can be comfortable in a more compact space. Keep in mind that all rabbits require a safe and secure area to live, as well as space to exercise and play. The perfect rabbit for your family will be one that fits comfortably in your home and has plenty of room to hop around and stretch their legs.

Step 3: Allergies and Sensitivities

Rabbits can be wonderful pets for people with allergies, as they don't produce the same allergens as cats and dogs. However, some people may still be sensitive to rabbit fur, hay, or bedding materials. If anyone in your family has allergies or sensitivities, it's important to spend time around rabbits and their living environment to make sure everyone can breathe easy and enjoy their new furry friend.

Step 4: A Bunny's Life

Rabbits are social creatures and need plenty of love and attention from their human family members. Before bringing a rabbit into your home, consider the time and commitment required to care for a bunny properly.

Rabbits need daily exercise, playtime, and interaction with their humans. They also require regular grooming, especially for long-haired breeds. The right rabbit for your family will be one that matches your schedule and lifestyle, ensuring that you have plenty of time to bond and create a lasting friendship.

Step 5: The Great Rabbit Meet-and-Greet

Once you've considered all the important factors, it's time to meet some rabbits! Visit local animal shelters, rescue organisations, or reputable breeders to interact with different bunnies. Remember, each rabbit is unique, and spending time with them will help you find the perfect match for your family.

When you meet a rabbit, take your time getting to know their personality. Are they friendly and outgoing, or more shy and reserved? Do they enjoy being petted and held, or do they prefer to explore and play? Pay attention to how each rabbit interacts with you and your family members, and trust your instincts when it comes to finding the right fit.

And there you have it, dear reader - our top tips to finding the perfect rabbit for your family. As you embark on this exciting journey, remember that the right rabbit is out there, just waiting to hop into your heart and home. With a little patience, love, and understanding, you'll soon welcome a fluffy new friend who will bring joy and happiness to your family for years to come. So hop to it, and may you find the rabbit of your dreams!

Chapter 4 - Loving Homes for Bunnies in Need

Rescuing or adopting a rabbit is a special way to show compassion and make a difference in a bunny's life. In this chapter, we will explore why rescuing or adopting rabbits is important, and guide you through the process. Get ready to discover how you can provide a loving home to a bunny who truly needs it!

1 - Why Rescuing and Adopting Matters

Saving Lives and Second Chances

When you rescue or adopt a rabbit, you're giving them a second chance at a happy life. Many rabbits in shelters or rescue organisations need a loving home, and by adopting, you're saving lives and making a real difference.

The Joy of Bonding and Companionship

Rescued rabbits often form deep bonds with their new families. They bring immense joy, love, and companionship to your life. By adopting, you have the chance to create a special connection with a bunny who needs your care and affection.

2 - Getting Ready to Rescue or Adopt

Assessing Your Lifestyle and Commitment

Before adopting a rabbit, it's important to think about your lifestyle and make sure you have the time, resources, and commitment needed to provide proper care. Rabbits have specific needs and can live for many years, so it's crucial to be ready for a long-term commitment.

Learning About Rabbit Care

Educate yourself about rabbit care, behaviour, and health needs. Understanding what rabbits eat, how they socialise, and the right living conditions will help you provide the best care for your adopted bunny.

Finding Reputable Rescue Organisations

Look for trustworthy rescue organisations in your area. These organisations prioritise the well-being of animals, have good facilities and guidelines, and promote responsible adoptions. You can ask local veterinarians, rabbit owners, or join online communities to find recommendations.

3 - The Adoption Journey

Making Initial Contact and Applying

Contact your chosen rescue organisation and ask about their adoption process. They might have an application form for you to fill out or an orientation session to help assess if you're a suitable adopter.

Home Visit and Evaluation

Some rescue organisations might visit your home to make sure it's a safe environment for a rabbit. They'll check things like safety measures, available space, and whether you have other pets.

Rescue organisations often charge adoption fees to cover the cost of caring for the rabbits. Take the time to review and understand the adoption agreement, which may include details about caring for the rabbit, their medical needs, and the organisation's return policies.

Meeting the Rabbits

Arrange a meeting with the rabbits available for adoption. Spend time with them, interact, and see if there's a connection. Consider their personality and how well they fit with your family and lifestyle.

Post-Adoption Support

Reputable rescue organisations offer support after adoption. They can provide guidance on rabbit care, behaviour, and health. Take advantage of these resources to ensure your adopted rabbit gets the best care possible.

Rescuing or adopting a rabbit is a wonderful way to make a positive impact in their lives. By understanding the importance of rescue and following the adoption process, you can provide a forever home to a bunny in need. Remember, your decision to adopt makes a significant difference for these amazing creatures.

Chapter 5 - Creating a Comfortable Living Space

There's nothing quite like the feeling of providing your rabbits with a cozy and secure home. As you embark on this exciting adventure, imagine a magical haven where your furry companions can hop, play, and snuggle to their heart's content. With a bit of creativity and love, you can create a paradise that your rabbits will adore.

Step 1: Understanding Rabbit Housing Needs

The first step to creating a rabbit haven is to learn about their needs and preferences. Rabbits are social creatures who crave attention and playtime. They also need a spacious and well-ventilated living space to thrive. Once you have a good understanding of your rabbits' needs, it's time to create a space that caters to their every desire.

Step 2: Choosing the Right Location

The location of your rabbit's living space is crucial to their health and happiness. It should be a quiet spot, away from loud noises and distractions. Consider placing their home in a peaceful corner of your backyard, near a garden filled with colourful flowers and lush greenery. This will provide them with a calming environment and fresh air. Once you've chosen the location, you can move on to selecting the perfect enclosure.

Step 3: Selecting the Right Enclosure

Rabbits need plenty of space to move and play, so choose an enclosure that is both roomy and well-ventilated. A large outdoor hutch with an attached run is an excellent option that allows your rabbits to have a cozy place to sleep and plenty of room to play during the day.

Step 4: Creating a Cozy and Welcoming Environment

Inside the hutch, create a welcoming environment by adding soft bedding made from hay and straw. This will provide your rabbits with a cozy spot to snuggle up and rest. Don't forget to add plenty of toys, tunnels, and hiding spots for your bunnies to explore and enjoy.

Step 5: Ensuring Proper Sanitation

Sanitation is also crucial for your rabbits' health and happiness. Place a litter box in one corner of the hutch and fill it with rabbit-friendly litter. This will make cleaning easier and keep their home smelling fresh and clean.

Step 6: Setting Up the Outdoor Run

Next, turn your attention to the outdoor run. Make sure it is secure, with no gaps or holes where your bunnies could escape or predators could enter. You can add a shade cover to protect your rabbits from the sun and a rain cover to keep them dry on rainy days. To make the run more engaging, include various toys and enrichment activities, such as logs and branches to climb and chew on, a digging box filled with soil for burrowing, and a variety of balls and treat dispensers.

Step 7: Adding Enrichment Activities

To make the run more exciting and engaging, add various toys and enrichment activities for your rabbits. Logs and branches for them to climb and chew on, a digging box filled with soil for them to dig and burrow in, and a variety of balls and treat dispensers will keep them entertained and stimulated.

Step 8: Regular Maintenance

Regular maintenance is essential to ensure your rabbits' living space is clean and safe. Check their hutch for any damages or potential hazards, clean their litter box daily, and replenish their bedding and hay as needed. Always keep an eye on your rabbits while they are outside in their run to ensure their safety.

Creating a rabbit haven is a journey filled with love and creativity. As you watch your rabbits hop, play, and snuggle in their cozy and secure home, you'll feel a sense of joy and pride knowing that you've provided them with the best possible life. So go ahead, create a rabbit paradise that your furry friends will adore!

Chapter 6 - Supplies and Equipment

Are you excited about the idea of bringing a cute, fluffy rabbit into your life? Rabbits make wonderful pets and companions, but they need the right supplies and equipment to stay happy, healthy, and hoppy! In this chapter, we'll explore all the essential items you'll need to create a comfortable and safe home for your new furry friend.

1. A Comfy, Cozy Home

To provide your rabbit with a suitable habitat, the first priority is to ensure it has a secure and comfortable living space. You can choose between a rabbit hutch, cage, or a spacious pen, making sure it is adequately sized for your bunny's needs.

It should be large enough for your rabbit to stretch out, stand upright on its hind legs, and hop around without constraint. As a general guideline, select a shelter that is at least four times the length of your fully stretched out rabbit and two times the width. This generous space will enable them to engage in playful activities, enjoy meals, and rest peacefully.

Make sure the hutch or cage has a solid floor, as wire floors can hurt your rabbit's sensitive feet. Add a soft bedding material, like hay or shredded paper, to keep your rabbit warm and cozy. Rabbits also appreciate having a private area in their home to hide away when they want some peace and quiet. A small cardboard box with a hole cut out for a door makes a perfect hiding spot!

2. Healthy Bunny Meals

Rabbits love munching on fresh hay, and it's an essential part of their diet. Be sure to provide unlimited hay for your rabbit to eat and nibble on throughout the day. You can use a hay rack or a clean litter box to keep the hay off the floor and clean.

In addition to hay, your rabbit will also need a small amount of high-quality rabbit pellets. These pellets contain important vitamins and minerals that keep your rabbit healthy. Be sure to follow the instructions on the pellet bag for how much to feed your rabbit based on their age and size.

Don't forget the veggies! Rabbits enjoy a variety of fresh, leafy greens, like lettuce, kale, and spinach. You can also offer them small amounts of other vegetables and fruits as treats. Just be sure to introduce new foods slowly and watch for any signs of an upset tummy.

3. Water, Water Everywhere

Hydration is key to keeping your rabbit healthy and happy. A water bottle with a metal spout or a sturdy ceramic bowl will work well for providing fresh water. Make sure to check the water level daily and clean the container regularly to prevent any buildup of bacteria.

4. Litter Box Training

Did you know that rabbits can be litter box trained? It's true! Providing your rabbit with a litter box will help keep their home clean and make it easier for you to care for them. Choose a litter box with low sides so your rabbit can hop in and out easily. Fill the box with a layer of rabbit-safe litter, like paper pellets or aspen shavings, and then add a layer of hay on top.

Place the litter box in a corner of the hutch or cage, as rabbits tend to do their business in one area. Be patient and give your rabbit some time to learn. With a little encouragement and positive reinforcement, they'll soon be using their litter box like a pro!

5. Toys for Fun and Enrichment

Rabbits are curious and intelligent animals, so they need toys and activities to keep them entertained and mentally stimulated. Offering a variety of toys will help prevent boredom and encourage your rabbit to stay active and engaged.

Chew toys are essential for rabbits, as their teeth grow continuously throughout their lives. Wooden blocks, cardboard tubes, and untreated wicker baskets make great chew toys. Just make sure the materials are safe and non-toxic.

Tunnels and hideaways are also popular with rabbits. They love exploring and having a quiet place to retreat to. You can buy tunnels specifically designed for rabbits or create your own using cardboard boxes or large PVC pipes.

6. Grooming Tools

Rabbits are generally clean animals and will groom themselves regularly. However, it's important to help them out by brushing their fur, especially during shedding season. A soft-bristle brush or a rubber grooming tool will work well for removing loose fur and keeping your rabbit's coat in tip-top shape.

Regular nail trims are also important. Rabbit nails can grow quite long and cause discomfort if not trimmed regularly. You can use a small pair of nail clippers designed for pets or ask your veterinarian to show you how to do it safely.

With these essential supplies and equipment, you'll be well-prepared to create a happy, hoppy home for your rabbit. Remember to always monitor your rabbit's health and well-being, and consult with a veterinarian if you have any concerns. By providing a safe and comfortable environment, a balanced diet, and plenty of love and attention, you'll enjoy many years of companionship with your furry friend.

Chapter 7 - Indoors vs. Outdoors

Once upon a time, in a world full of fluffy and furry little creatures, there were rabbits. Rabbits of all shapes, sizes, and colours, hopping around their homes and exploring their surroundings. Some rabbits lived indoors, spending their days roaming through the cozy rooms of their human family's home. Other rabbits lived outdoors, hopping through the grassy fields, and basking in the warm sunshine. But which is better for a rabbit: living indoors or outdoors? That is the great debate we shall explore today, my dear friends!

Indoor Rabbits

First, let's hop on over to the indoor rabbit's world. Imagine this: A soft, warm carpet beneath your little paws, and the delightful scent of freshly baked cookies wafting through the air. The indoor rabbit spends their days exploring the many nooks and crannies of their human home. They may even have their very own room, complete with a comfy bed, toys to play with, and a little corner for nibbling on their favourite hay and veggies.

Living indoors has many advantages for rabbits. For one, they are protected from the harsh weather conditions and predators that may lurk in the great outdoors. Indoor rabbits don't have to worry about such dangers, as they are safe and sound within the shelter of their human's home.

Furthermore, indoor rabbits are more likely to receive regular attention from their human family members. This means more pats, more cuddles, and more love! Who wouldn't want that? Spending time with humans also helps rabbits become more social and friendly, making them wonderful companions for people of all ages.

However, living indoors also has its challenges. For example, rabbits may be tempted to nibble on the furniture, electrical cords, or even the wallpaper! Oh, dear! It's essential for indoor rabbits to have plenty of toys and safe chewing alternatives to keep them entertained and out of trouble. Rabbits also need space to hop, run, and stretch their legs, so a roomy enclosure or play area is a must for any indoor bunny.

Pros

Protected from harsh weather conditions and predators

More likely to receive regular attention and social interaction from their human family members

May be easier to litter box train

Can be less noisy and chaotic than outdoor living

May be tempted to nibble on furniture and household items

Need plenty of toys and safe chewing alternatives to keep them entertained and out of trouble

Need space to hop, run, and stretch their legs, so a roomy enclosure or play area is a must

Outdoor Rabbits

Now, let's bounce over to the outdoor rabbit's world. Picture this: Green grass beneath your paws, the warm sun shining on your fur, and the sweet sound of birds singing in the trees. The outdoor rabbit has an entirely different experience than their indoor counterpart. They have plenty of space to roam and explore, with the freedom to dig, graze on grass, and bask in the sunlight to their heart's content.

Outdoor rabbits can live in a spacious hutch or enclosure, complete with hiding spots, tunnels, and a cozy sleeping area to snuggle up in during the night. Living outdoors allows rabbits to experience the natural world, which can be stimulating and enriching for their curious little minds.

However, living outdoors also comes with its fair share of risks. Rabbits are prey animals, and the great outdoors can be a dangerous place for them. They must be protected from predators, such as foxes, raccoons, and birds of prey, by having a secure and sturdy enclosure. Furthermore, outdoor rabbits must be kept safe from extreme weather conditions, such as heat, cold, and rain, which may require additional shelter, heaters, or insulation.

Outdoor rabbits may not receive as much attention and social interaction from their human family members as indoor rabbits do. This can make them more timid and less social, which may not be ideal for those looking for a cuddly companion. To ensure that outdoor rabbits remain friendly and well-socialised, it's important to spend quality time with them regularly, providing plenty of love and attention.

Pros

Plenty of space to roam and explore, with the freedom to dig, graze on grass, and bask in the sunlight

Can experience the natural world, which can be stimulating and enriching for their curious minds

Can be less expensive than indoor living, as rabbits can graze on grass instead of hay

Cons

Must be protected from predators, such as foxes, raccoons, and birds of prey, by having a secure and sturdy enclosure

Must be kept safe from extreme weather conditions, such as heat, cold, and rain, which may require additional shelter or insulation

May not receive as much attention and social interaction from their human family members as indoor rabbits do, making them more timid and less social

So, my dear rabbit-loving friends, the great debate continues! Is it better for rabbits to live indoors or outdoors? The truth is, both options have their pros and cons, and the best choice for your rabbit will depend on your unique circumstances and your rabbit's personality. What's most important is that your rabbit is provided with a safe, comfortable, and loving home, whether it be inside your cozy abode or in the great outdoors.

No matter where your rabbit lives, always remember to give them plenty of love, attention, and care. By doing so, you'll be rewarded with a happy, healthy, and hoppy companion who will fill your life with joy and wonder. And that, my friends, is the true magic of sharing your life with a rabbit.

Chapter 8 - Keeping Rabbits Outdoors

The Joy of Outdoor Living

Rabbits are natural outdoor creatures, and providing them with a safe and enriching outdoor living space can enhance their well-being and happiness. However, it's important to be aware of the challenges posed by extreme weather conditions and take necessary measures to ensure their comfort and safety.

Understanding Extreme Weather

Extreme heat and cold can pose risks to rabbits, so it's crucial to understand the potential dangers and how to mitigate them. Here are some key considerations:

Hot Weather Precautions

Rabbits are susceptible to heat stress, which can be life-threatening. Here's what you can do to protect your outdoor rabbits during hot weather:

Providing Shade

Ensure that your rabbit's outdoor area has ample shade to protect them from direct sunlight. Use natural shade from trees or create artificial shade using umbrellas, tarps, or specially designed shades.

Proper Ventilation

Good airflow is essential to keep rabbits cool. Make sure there's sufficient air circulation in their living space. You can use fans or provide well-ventilated housing options.

Fresh Water

Offer cool and fresh water to your rabbits at all times, especially during hot weather. Check their water sources frequently to ensure they are clean and filled.

Frozen Treats

Help your rabbits stay cool by offering them frozen treats like ice cubes or frozen vegetables. These can provide relief from the heat and be a fun source of enrichment.

Cold Weather Preparations

Rabbits are susceptible to the cold and can suffer from hypothermia or frostbite. Here's how you can protect your outdoor rabbits during cold weather:

Providing Insulation

Ensure that your rabbit's outdoor hutch or enclosure is well-insulated to retain heat. Use materials like straw or blankets to create a cozy and warm environment.

Wind Protection

Protect your rabbits from cold winds by using windbreakers or positioning their enclosure in a sheltered area. This helps prevent drafts and keeps them comfortable.

Extra Bedding

Add extra bedding to your rabbit's living space during colder months to provide additional insulation and warmth. Consider using straw or hay to create a cozy nesting area.

Warm Water and Food

Provide your rabbits with warm water and fresh, nutrient-rich food during colder days. This helps maintain their body temperature and supports their overall health.

Regular Monitoring and Care

Keeping rabbits outdoors requires regular monitoring and care. Here are some important aspects to consider:

1. Daily Checks

Perform daily checks to ensure your rabbits have access to fresh water, appropriate shelter, and a clean living space. Monitor their behaviour, eating habits, and overall well-being.

2. Weather Updates

Stay informed about weather forecasts and be prepared to make necessary adjustments based on changing weather conditions. This allows you to take proactive steps to protect your rabbits.

3. Veterinary Care

Schedule regular veterinary check-ups for your outdoor rabbits. A qualified veterinarian can provide guidance on their specific needs and address any health concerns that may arise.

Enjoying the Outdoors Safely

With proper precautions and care, your rabbits can enjoy the outdoors safely. Outdoor living provides them with opportunities for exercise, exploration, and natural behaviours. By following the guidelines and being attentive to their well-being, you can create a safe and enriching outdoor environment for your rabbits. Here are some additional tips to ensure their well-being:

1. Regular Exercise

Allow your rabbits ample space for exercise and play in their outdoor enclosure. Provide tunnels, ramps, and toys to stimulate their natural instincts and keep them physically active.

2. Predator Protection

Take precautions to protect your rabbits from potential predators. Ensure their enclosure has secure fencing and a sturdy roof to prevent access from larger animals or birds of prey. Regularly inspect the enclosure for any gaps or vulnerabilities.

3. Avoid Harmful Plants

Be mindful of the plants in your rabbit's outdoor area. Some plants can be toxic to rabbits if ingested. Research rabbit-safe plants and avoid those that may pose a risk. Provide plenty of rabbit-friendly greens instead.

4. Social Interaction

Spend time with your rabbits outdoors, engaging in gentle interaction and bonding activities. This can include sitting near their enclosure, talking softly to them, or offering treats. Building a strong bond through positive socialisation is essential for their emotional well-being.

5. Supervised Exploration

Allow your rabbits supervised access to a secure, rabbit-proofed outdoor space beyond their enclosure. This controlled exploration time allows them to experience different textures, smells, and sights while ensuring their safety.

6. Monitor Temperature Changes

Keep a close eye on temperature changes throughout the day, especially during transitional seasons. Provide additional bedding or adjust their living space accordingly to maintain a comfortable temperature for your rabbits.

Remember, responsible outdoor rabbit keeping involves regular monitoring, adjustments, and a commitment to their well-being. By providing a safe, comfortable, and stimulating environment, you can ensure that your rabbits enjoy the benefits of outdoor living while keeping them protected from extreme weather conditions and potential dangers.

Keeping rabbits outdoors can be a wonderful experience for both you and your furry companions. By following the guidelines outlined in this chapter, you can provide a safe and enjoyable outdoor environment where your rabbits can thrive. With proper awareness of extreme weather conditions and a commitment to their care, you can create a harmonious and fulfilling outdoor living arrangement for your beloved rabbits.

Chapter 9 - Rabbit-Proofing Your Home

Rabbit-proofing your home is an essential step in ensuring the safety and happiness of your furry friend. Rabbits are curious creatures that love to explore and nibble on anything that catches their eye. However, this can sometimes get them into trouble, especially in a home filled with potential hazards. To ensure that your bunny stays safe and happy, it's important to take the necessary steps to rabbit-proof your home.

1: The Great Wall of Bunny Safety

Rabbits are natural explorers, with an insatiable curiosity that often gets them into trouble. But fear not! By creating a special play area for your beloved bunny, you can provide them with a safe and secure space to hop, jump, and nibble to their heart's content.

There are a few options for creating a bunny-proof barrier around your bunny's play area. Baby gates and playpens are a popular choice, and are perfect for keeping your bunny out of harm's way. For larger play areas, pet exercise pens or wire mesh fencing are ideal options. Just make sure that whatever barrier you choose is tall and sturdy enough to keep your bunny from escaping and durable enough to withstand their natural urge to chew and scratch.

While a bunny-proof barrier is a great first step in keeping your bunny safe, it's important to remember that it's not a substitute for supervision. Keep a watchful eye on your furry friend and make sure they're not attempting to jump over or gnaw through the barrier.

With a designated play area, you can give your bunny the freedom to explore and play to their heart's content, all while ensuring that they stay out of harm's way.

2: Rabbit-Proof Cables

To ensure the safety of your bunny, it's essential to cover all electrical cables and cords to prevent your furry friend from chewing on them. These seemingly harmless items can pose serious threats to rabbits, causing injuries or even death if ingested. Thankfully, you can use plastic tubing or cord protectors that are specifically designed for this purpose to avoid any potential accidents. These lifesaving accessories can be easily purchased at most pet stores or online.

In addition to covering cables, it's equally important to keep electronics out of your bunny's reach to avoid any curiosity-driven nibbling. Items such as televisions, speakers, and lamps should be placed out of your bunny's access. Make sure to secure any loose cords or wires too, as they can be just as hazardous as electrical cables. Don't let your bunny's inquisitiveness lead to harm, take the necessary precautions to ensure their safety.

With their natural tendency to nibble on anything that catches their eye, it's important to safeguard them against potential hazards. Chemical cleaners, paints, and certain plants can be toxic to rabbits if ingested, and harsh cleaning products can harm their delicate respiratory systems.

To keep your bunny safe, take precautions by storing all hazardous items out of their reach, ideally in a locked cabinet or on a high shelf. Swap out any toxic plants for rabbit-friendly alternatives and consult with your veterinarian or local pet store for a list of safe and unsafe plants for your bunny.

When cleaning your home, be mindful of the products you use. Avoid using chemicals that can irritate your bunny's respiratory system, and opt for natural cleaning solutions like vinegar and baking soda. Make sure to clean your bunny's living area in a different room or enclosure to prevent them from inhaling any harmful fumes or particles.

By taking these necessary steps and being aware of potential hazards, you can create a safe and healthy environment for your bunny to thrive in, allowing them to explore and play to their heart's content.

4: The Wonderful World of Toys

Rabbits are social animals and love to play and explore. Providing your bunny with plenty of bunny-safe toys is not only important in preventing boredom but can also help keep them physically and mentally healthy. Chew toys made of untreated wood, cardboard, and sisal are great for promoting healthy teeth and satisfying your bunny's urge to chew. Puzzle toys, such as treat balls or toys with hidden compartments, provide mental stimulation and can help prevent destructive behaviour.

In addition to providing a variety of toys, it's also important to regularly rotate them to keep your bunny interested and engaged. You can also make DIY toys at home using items like toilet paper rolls, cardboard boxes, and hay-filled baskets.

However, be sure to avoid any materials that could be harmful to your bunny, such as plastic or glue.

Remember, a happy and entertained bunny is less likely to become destructive and explore areas that may be harmful to them. By providing your bunny with plenty of bunny-safe toys, you can help keep them physically and mentally healthy while also protecting your home.

5: Soft and Cozy Floors

Rabbits need traction to be able to move around safely and confidently. Slippery floors can cause rabbits to slip and fall, leading to injuries such as sprains or broken bones. To prevent these accidents, it's important to provide your bunny with a soft and cozy surface to walk on.

Placing rugs or mats on slippery floors can provide the necessary traction for your bunny to move around safely. Rugs also offer a comfortable and cozy area for your bunny to rest and play. Choose rugs that are easy to clean and avoid materials that your bunny may chew on, such as wool or synthetic fibres.

If your home has a lot of slippery floors or your bunny has mobility issues, you may want to consider installing non-slip flooring options such as rubber mats. These options provide a textured surface that allows your bunny to move around with ease while also being easy to clean and maintain.

Overall, the type of flooring you choose for your bunny's living space is important for their safety and comfort. By providing a soft and cozy surface with adequate traction, you can help prevent accidents and keep your bunny happy and healthy.

Rabbit-proofing your home is an important aspect of being a responsible bunny enthusiast. By taking the necessary steps to create a safe and comfortable environment for your furry friend, you can ensure that they are happy and healthy while also protecting them from potential hazards. From creating barriers and covering electrical cables to being mindful of household items and providing plenty of bunny-safe toys and soft, cozy flooring, there are many ways to rabbit-proof your home. By following the tips outlined in this chapter, you can create a safe and enjoyable living space for your bunny and enjoy your time together without worrying about their safety.

Chapter 10 - Outdoor Rabbit Runs

Rabbits love exploring the great outdoors - the fresh air, sunshine, and soft grass are simply irresistible. However, outdoor playtime can come with risks. That's where the Outdoor Rabbit Run comes in. With a little bit of effort and creativity, you can create a safe and fun environment for your bunny to hop and play to their heart's content. So let's dive in and discover the secrets to creating the perfect outdoor rabbit run for your furry friend!

Outdoor Rabbit Runs

Imagine an enchanted garden filled with beautiful flowers, tall grasses, and shady trees. This is the world of outdoor rabbit runs - a place where bunnies can run, play, and explore safely. But creating this magical space takes time, effort, and lots of love.

To make the perfect outdoor rabbit run, you'll need a few key ingredients. First, you need a strong and secure fence to keep your bunny safe from any dangers that might be lurking outside. This fence should be tall enough so that your rabbit can't jump over it, and it should also have a roof or netting to protect them from any curious birds that might swoop down for a visit. You'll also need a gate or door so that you can easily get in and out of the rabbit run.

Next, you'll want to add some fun and engaging toys for your bunny to play with. These can include tunnels, ramps, and even a digging box filled with sand or soil. The more exciting the toys, the more your rabbit will enjoy their outdoor adventure!

Lastly, don't forget to provide a shady spot for your rabbit to rest and relax. A small hideaway or shelter will make the perfect spot for your bunny to take a break from all their hopping and playing.

Outdoor Rabbit Safety

While the world of outdoor rabbit runs is a fun and exciting place, it's also important to remember that there are some dangers lurking in the shadows. To keep your rabbit safe and sound, you'll need to be aware of these potential hazards.

One of the most common dangers in the outdoors is predators. These sneaky creatures might try to find a way into your rabbit run to cause harm to your furry friend. To keep your bunny safe, make sure your fence is secure and that there are no gaps or holes that a predator could sneak through. It's also a good idea to check the rabbit run regularly for any signs of damage or wear.

Another danger that might be hiding in your rabbit run is poisonous plants. Some plants, like foxgloves and lilies, can be harmful to rabbits if they eat them. To prevent any accidents, make sure you know which plants are safe for rabbits and remove any toxic plants from the area.

Lastly, the sun can also pose a threat to your rabbit's health. On hot days, rabbits can become overheated if they don't have a place to cool down. Make sure to provide plenty of shade and fresh water for your bunny to keep them happy and healthy.

The Magical Bond Between You and Your Rabbit

One of the most wonderful things about having an outdoor rabbit run is the special bond it can create between you and your bunny. Spending time together outside can help strengthen your relationship and make your rabbit feel more comfortable and happy.

To make the most of your time in the rabbit run, try to visit your bunny at least once a day. This will help them get used to your presence and make them more likely to approach you for cuddles and pets. You can also try hand-feeding your rabbit some of their favourite treats to encourage them to come closer.

Another great way to bond with your rabbit is to play with them. Try creating some fun games, like hiding treats around the rabbit run for them to find or rolling a small ball for them to chase. The more you interact with your rabbit, the stronger your bond will become.

Did you know that rabbits are super smart? They have curious minds and love to explore and discover new things. Just like us, they need mental stimulation to prevent boredom and stay happy and healthy. That's where environmental enrichment comes in!

Environmental enrichment means creating an exciting and stimulating environment for your rabbit. It's like setting up a playground just for them! One way to do this is by providing toys that they can chew, toss, and play with. Rabbits love toys made from safe materials like wood, cardboard, or even special rabbit-safe plastic. You can find these toys at pet stores or even make some yourself!

But toys are just the beginning. Rabbits also love to explore, so why not create a little adventure land for them? You can set up tunnels made from sturdy materials like PVC pipes or cardboard tubes. Rabbits will have a blast hopping in and out, discovering hidden nooks and crannies. You can even create obstacle courses using boxes or old blankets. It's like setting up a rabbit Olympics!

Another way to keep your rabbit's mind active is by providing them with safe objects to chew on. Rabbits have special teeth that grow continuously, and they need to chew to keep them healthy. You can offer them safe chew sticks made from apple or willow wood. These not only provide entertainment but also help wear down their teeth. Just make sure the sticks are free from any harmful chemicals or pesticides.

Don't forget the power of nature! Rabbits love to explore the great outdoors, but it's important to keep them safe. You can create a secure outdoor playpen or even a supervised indoor garden with rabbit-friendly plants. This way, they can enjoy fresh air, nibble on grass or dandelions, and experience new smells and textures. Remember to always supervise them during outdoor playtime to keep them safe from predators or harmful plants.

Now, let's talk about the power of your presence. Rabbits are social animals and enjoy spending time with their human friends. They love gentle strokes and being talked to softly. Spending time with your rabbit, playing and interacting with them, is an excellent form of mental enrichment. It helps strengthen your bond and keeps them emotionally happy.

Remember, every rabbit is unique, so try different toys and activities to see what they enjoy the most. Rotate their toys and change their play area from time to time to keep things fresh and exciting. And always make sure the toys and objects are safe and free from any small parts that could be swallowed.

By providing environmental enrichment, you're giving your rabbit a happy and exciting life. Their minds will stay sharp, and they'll have plenty of fun exploring, playing, and bonding with you. So, get creative, set up a rabbit wonderland, and watch your furry friend hop, binky, and play to their heart's content!

A Hoppy Ending

With a little bit of love, care, and attention, you can create the perfect outdoor rabbit run for your furry friend and enjoy countless hoppy adventures together.

So, as you embark on this exciting journey, keep these important lessons in mind: create a safe and secure space for your bunny, be aware of any potential dangers, and cherish the special bond between you and your rabbit. With these ingredients, you'll have a recipe for a happy, healthy, and hoppy life with your beloved bunny.

Did you know that rabbits are super smart? They have curious minds and love to explore and discover new things. Just like us, they need mental stimulation to prevent boredom and stay happy and healthy. That's where environmental enrichment comes in!

Toys

Environmental enrichment means creating an exciting and stimulating environment for your rabbit. It's like setting up a playground just for them! One way to do this is by providing toys that they can chew, toss, and play with. Rabbits love toys made from safe materials like wood, cardboard, or even special rabbit-safe plastic. You can find these toys at pet stores or even make some yourself!

Create a Bunny Obstacle Course

But toys are just the beginning. Rabbits also love to explore, so why not create a little adventure land for them? You can set up tunnels made from sturdy materials like PVC pipes or cardboard tubes. Rabbits will have a blast hopping in and out, discovering hidden nooks and crannies. You can even create obstacle courses using boxes or old blankets. It's like setting up a rabbit Olympics!

Rabbits Love to Chew

Another way to keep your rabbit's mind active is by providing them with safe objects to chew on. Rabbits have special teeth that grow continuously, and they need to chew to keep them healthy. You can offer them safe chew sticks made from apple or willow wood. These not only provide entertainment but also help wear down their teeth. Just make sure the sticks are free from any harmful chemicals or pesticides.

Outdoor Playtime

Don't forget the power of nature! Rabbits love to explore the great outdoors, but it's important to keep them safe. You can create a secure outdoor playpen or even a supervised indoor garden with rabbit-friendly plants. This way, they can enjoy fresh air, nibble on grass or dandelions, and experience new smells and textures. Remember to always supervise them during outdoor playtime to keep them safe from predators or harmful plants.

Strokes and Cuddle Time

Now, let's talk about the power of your presence. Rabbits are social animals and enjoy spending time with their human friends. They love gentle strokes and being talked to softly. Spending time with your rabbit, playing and interacting with them, is an excellent form of mental enrichment. It helps strengthen your bond and keeps them emotionally happy.

Remember, every rabbit is unique, so try different toys and activities to see what they enjoy the most. Rotate their toys and change their play area from time to time to keep things fresh and exciting. And always make sure the toys and objects are safe and free from any small parts that could be swallowed.

By providing environmental enrichment, you're giving your rabbit a happy and exciting life. Their minds will stay sharp, and they'll have plenty of fun exploring, playing, and bonding with you. So, get creative, set up a rabbit wonderland, and watch your furry friend hop, binky, and play to their heart's content!

Chapter 12 - Rabbit Food

Welcome to the wonderful world of rabbit food, where a balanced and varied diet is the key to keeping your furry friend healthy and happy. As natural herbivores, rabbits require a diet that consists mainly of hay, vegetables, and fruits. These foods provide essential nutrients that keep their digestive system functioning properly and their teeth healthy. In this chapter, we will explore the different types of hay, vegetables, and fruits that rabbits love to eat, and learn how to create a menu that provides the right balance of nutrients for your bunny. So, let's dive into the wonderful world of rabbit food and discover what makes our furry friends hop with joy during mealtime!

Hopping into Hay

Hay is the most important food in a rabbit's diet, as it keeps their tummies happy and their teeth in tip-top shape, hay should be available all day, every day. This is because hay helps maintain their digestive health and keeps their teeth in good condition. A constant supply of hay is like a magical potion that keeps them strong and active.

There are many types of hay, each with its own unique taste and texture. Let's explore some of the most popular hays that rabbits love to nibble on!

1.   Timothy Hay

Timothy hay is a favourite among rabbits and is often considered the best hay for their health. It has a sweet, earthy aroma that makes rabbits' noses wiggle with excitement. Timothy hay comes in three different cuts, each with varying levels of stems, leaves, and seed heads. The first cut is the crunchiest, while the third cut is the softest and leafiest. Rabbits love all cuts of Timothy hay, and it provides the perfect balance of fibre and nutrients to keep them healthy and strong.

2.   Orchard Grass Hay

Orchard grass hay is another excellent choice for rabbits. Its soft, sweet taste makes it a delightful treat for our furry friends.

Orchard grass hay is lower in protein and calcium than Timothy hay, making it an ideal option for older rabbits or those with special dietary needs.

3. Meadow Hay

Meadow hay is a mix of various grasses and plants, offering rabbits a diverse and delightful smorgasbord of flavours and textures. Each mouthful is a new adventure, keeping rabbits engaged and entertained during mealtime. Meadow hay is a great option for rabbits who enjoy a little variety in their diet.

Veggie Wonderland

Vegetables are a vital part of a rabbit's diet, providing essential vitamins and minerals that keep them healthy and energetic. Rabbits love to munch on a wide variety of veggies, making mealtime a colourful and exciting experience.

Providing your rabbit with a variety of vegetables every day, such as leafy greens, carrots, bell peppers, and broccoli, is crucial for maintaining a balanced diet. It is recommended that a rabbit should eat one cup of vegetables for every two pounds of body weight daily. However, it is essential to introduce new vegetables slowly and one at a time to prevent stomach upset.

Here are some popular vegetables that rabbits adore:

1. Leafy Greens: The Majestic Forest of Flavour

Leafy greens, such as romaine lettuce, kale, and Swiss chard, are the royalty of the vegetable world. Their tender leaves and crisp stems provide a delightful crunch that rabbits find irresistible. Leafy greens should make up the majority of a rabbit's vegetable intake, as they are low in calories and high in nutrients.

2. Bell Peppers: The Jester of Joy

Bell peppers, in all their vibrant colours, add a touch of whimsy to a rabbit's meal. Their sweet, crunchy texture makes them a delightful treat for rabbits to nibble on. Bell peppers are an excellent source of vitamin C, an essential nutrient for our furry friends.

Broccoli may look like miniature trees, but they pack a powerful punch of flavour and nutrients. Rabbits love to munch on the tender florets and crunchy stalks, making broccoli a fun and healthy addition to their diet.

Pellets

Pellets are an excellent source of essential nutrients, including protein and fibre, that rabbits need to maintain their health. However, it's crucial to keep in mind that pellets should be used as a supplement to hay and vegetables, not as the primary source of nutrition. Too many pellets can lead to obesity, which can cause various health issues, including heart disease and digestive problems.

When selecting pellets for your rabbit, opt for high-quality pellets that contain at least 18% fibre and are free from added sugars or fillers. Pellets that are high in fibre can help prevent health issues like hairballs and gut stasis, which can be life-threatening to rabbits.

It's important to remember that a rabbit's pellet intake should be based on their weight. For every four pounds of body weight, a rabbit should eat approximately 1/4 cup of pellets daily. However, it's essential to monitor your rabbit's weight and adjust their pellet intake accordingly. If your rabbit is gaining weight, reduce their pellet intake and increase their hay and vegetable intake.

Feeding your rabbit pellets in moderation can help prevent health problems and keep your rabbit healthy and happy. Remember to always provide a variety of hay, vegetables, and pellets, and offer treats in moderation to ensure your rabbit's diet is well-balanced.

Fruitful Delights

Fruits are the dessert of the rabbit world, offering a sweet and juicy treat for our furry friends. However, fruits should be fed in moderation, as their high sugar content can lead to an upset tummy if fed in large amounts. Here are some fruits that rabbits find simply irresistible:

Apples

Apples are a classic favourite among rabbits, with their sweet, juicy flesh and crunchy texture. Rabbits love to nibble on apple slices, making them a perfect treat for special occasions. Just remember to remove the seeds, as they can be harmful to rabbits.

Strawberries

Strawberries are like precious gems in the world of rabbit food, offering a sweet and tangy burst of flavour that rabbits adore. Their vibrant red colour and heart-shaped form make them a beautiful addition to any rabbit's meal. Strawberries are also packed with vitamin C, making them a healthy and delicious treat.

Blueberries

Blueberries may be small, but they are mighty in flavour and nutrients. Their sweet, juicy taste makes them a favourite among rabbits, who love to gobble up these tiny treats. Blueberries are also a great source of antioxidants, which help keep rabbits healthy and strong.

Foods to Avoid

While it's important to know what foods are safe and healthy for your rabbit to eat, it's equally important to be aware of what foods should be avoided. Here are some things to keep in mind when feeding your furry friend:

High Starch and High Sugar Foods

Rabbits have sensitive digestive systems and cannot properly digest foods that are high in starch and sugar. These foods can cause digestive upset, leading to diarrhea and other health problems. Foods to avoid include cereal, bread, crackers, pasta, and sugary treats.

Dairy Products

Rabbits are lactose intolerant, which means they cannot digest milk or other dairy products properly. Feeding your rabbit dairy products can cause digestive upset, leading to diarrhea and other health problems.

Foods High in Fat

Rabbits require a low-fat diet, as their bodies are not designed to handle large amounts of fat. Feeding your rabbit foods that are high in fat, such as nuts and seeds, can lead to obesity, digestive problems, and other health issues.

Cruciferous Vegetables

While vegetables are an important part of a rabbit's diet, certain vegetables should be avoided in large quantities. Cruciferous vegetables, such as cabbage, broccoli, and cauliflower, contain compounds that can cause gas and digestive upset in rabbits.

Avocado: Avocado is toxic to rabbits and can cause respiratory distress, fluid accumulation around the heart, and even death.

Chocolate and Caffeine

Chocolate and caffeine are toxic to rabbits and can cause heart problems, seizures, and even death. These should be avoided at all costs.

By being mindful of what foods to avoid, you can help keep your rabbit healthy and happy. Stick to a diet of hay, vegetables, and fruits, and always consult with your veterinarian if you have any questions or concerns about your rabbit's diet.

The magical garden of rabbit food is filled with a diverse and delightful array of hays, vegetables, and fruits. By offering our furry friends a balanced and varied diet, we can ensure they stay healthy, happy, and hoppy for years to come. So, let's celebrate the wonderful world of rabbit food and remember to always feed our rabbits with love and care!

Chapter 13 - Handling & Bonding with Your Bunny

Rabbits are wonderful companions, and building a strong bond with them requires proper handling and socialisation. In this chapter, we will explore helpful tips and guidance on how to handle, socialise, and bond with rabbits. Whether you're a new rabbit owner or looking to improve your relationship with your furry friend, get ready to discover the secrets of creating a deep and loving connection.

The Basics of Safe Handling

Proper handling is essential to ensure the safety and well-being of both you and your rabbit.

Follow these tips for a safe and comfortable handling experience:

- Approach your rabbit calmly and gently, allowing them to see and sniff your hand before attempting to pick them up.

- Support their body by placing one hand under their chest and the other hand under their hindquarters.

- Lift your rabbit slowly and confidently, keeping them close to your body to provide a sense of security.

- Avoid lifting them by their ears or pulling on their fur, as this can cause discomfort or injury.

- Always supervise children when they are handling rabbits to ensure gentle and respectful interactions.

Building Trust and Bonding

Creating a strong bond with your rabbit requires time, patience, and understanding.

Follow these steps to build trust and deepen your connection:

- Spend time sitting near your rabbit's living area, allowing them to approach you at their own pace.

- Offer tasty treats or their favourite vegetables as a reward for positive interactions and to associate your presence with something enjoyable.

- Talk to your rabbit in a soft, soothing voice, using their name to help them become familiar with you.

- Provide gentle strokes and scratches in areas your rabbit enjoys, such as behind the ears or under the chin.

- Engage in interactive play sessions using toys or gentle games like rolling a ball or hiding treats for them to find.

Socialising with Other Pets

Introducing your rabbit to other pets in the household requires careful management and gradual introductions.

Follow these steps to ensure a smooth and positive socialisation process:

- Start by allowing your rabbit and the other pet to become familiar with each other's scents by swapping bedding or using a barrier like a baby gate.

- Gradually introduce them in a controlled and supervised environment, such as a neutral space where neither pet feels territorial.

- Watch for signs of stress or aggression from either pet and be ready to separate them if needed.

- Reward positive interactions and provide separate safe spaces for each pet to retreat to when they need a break.

Remember that each pet is unique, and the introduction process may take time. Be patient and continue to monitor their interactions until a harmonious relationship develops.

Respecting Boundaries and Individual Personalities

Just like humans, rabbits have unique personalities and preferences. It's important to respect their boundaries and allow them to dictate their comfort level during interactions.

Here are some key points to keep in mind:

- Pay attention to your rabbit's body language, such as flattened ears, thumping, or attempting to move away. These signs indicate they may feel uncomfortable or stressed.

- Avoid forcing your rabbit into interactions they are not ready for. Give them space and time to feel secure and approach you on their terms.

- Understand that not all rabbits enjoy being held or cuddled. Some may prefer to be close to you without physical contact or enjoy being stroked while staying on the ground.

- Respect your rabbit's need for rest and downtime. Provide them with a quiet, comfortable area where they can retreat and relax when they want to be alone.

Handling and socialisation are key aspects of building a strong and loving bond with your bunny friends. By following proper handling techniques, building trust through positive interactions, and respecting their individual personalities and boundaries, you can create a deep and meaningful connection with your rabbits. Remember to be patient, understanding, and always prioritise their comfort and well-being. With time and effort, you'll develop a beautiful relationship filled with joy, trust, and companionship. Enjoy the journey of bonding with your furry friends and cherish the special moments you share together.

Chapter 14 - Rabbit Grooming

In the world of rabbits, grooming is a very important ritual, and brushing and trimming their fur is an essential part of this process. When you have a rabbit as a pet, you hold the key to unlocking the magic of grooming. So let's hop to it and learn all about the wonderful world of rabbit grooming: brushing and trimming their fur.

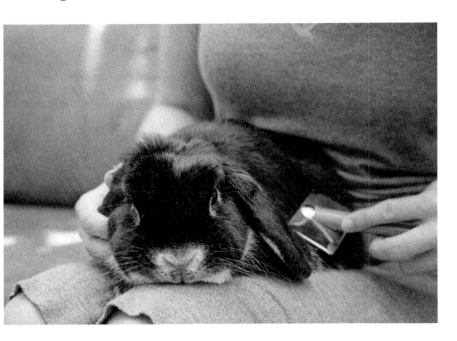

Before we begin our journey into grooming, it's important to know that rabbits have very sensitive skin. This means that we must be extra gentle and careful when brushing and trimming their fur. With love, patience, and a bit of practice, you'll soon become a master at keeping your rabbit's fur looking fabulous.

Brushing

First things first, let's talk about brushing. Just like how we brush our hair to keep it tidy and free from tangles, rabbits also need their fur to be brushed regularly. Regular brushing helps to remove loose fur, prevent mats from forming, and keep your rabbit's coat shiny and soft.

When it comes to selecting the perfect brush for your rabbit, there are a few things to consider. You'll want to choose a brush that is gentle on your rabbit's skin, easy to hold, and effective at removing loose fur. Some popular options include slicker brushes, bristle brushes, and rubber grooming gloves. Don't be afraid to try out different brushes and see which one works best for your rabbit. The world of rabbit grooming is full of surprises, and there's always more to learn!

Now that we've chosen our grooming tool, it's time to start brushing. Find a quiet and comfortable spot for you and your rabbit to sit. Gently hold your rabbit in your lap or let them sit beside you. Remember, rabbits can be a bit nervous, so always approach them with love and patience.

Begin by gently stroking your rabbit's fur to help them relax and get used to the sensation of being groomed. Once your rabbit seems comfortable, slowly start brushing their fur in the direction it naturally grows. Be sure to use gentle, short strokes and avoid pulling on any tangles or mats. If you come across a stubborn tangle, don't worry - we'll talk about how to handle those in just a bit!

As you lovingly brush your rabbit's fur, you might notice something magical happening. With each stroke, you're building a strong bond between you and your rabbit. This bond, filled with trust and love, is what makes grooming such a special time for both of you.

Dealing with Mats and Tangles

Despite regular brushing, mats and tangles can sometimes form, particularly in longer-haired breeds. It's essential to address these promptly as they can cause discomfort and even lead to skin infections. Never attempt to pull a mat apart with your fingers as this can cause pain and potentially injure the rabbit's sensitive skin.

To remove a mat, use a mat splitter or a pair of small, sharp scissors. Hold the mat at the base to avoid pulling the skin and carefully cut through the mat, aiming to keep the scissors parallel to the skin to prevent any accidental nicks. Always trim a little at a time; it's better to be safe than sorry. In case of uncertainty, consult a professional groomer or a veterinarian.

Trimming

Now let's talk about trimming. While brushing helps to keep your rabbit's fur looking fabulous, sometimes they may need a little trim to remove any mats or tangles that have formed. Trimming can also help to prevent fur from getting dirty or soiled, especially around their bottom area.

To trim your rabbit's fur, you'll need a pair of small, sharp scissors. Remember, safety first! Make sure to always keep your fingers between the scissors and your rabbit's skin to prevent any accidents. It's also a good idea to have a friend or family member help you hold your rabbit during the trimming process.

To trim a mat or tangle, gently hold the fur between your fingers and carefully snip away the affected area. Be sure to only trim small amounts at a time to avoid accidentally cutting too close to your rabbit's skin. If you're unsure or nervous about

71

trimming your rabbit's fur, don't hesitate to ask for help from an experienced rabbit groomer or your veterinarian.

Bathing

Contrary to popular belief, rabbits rarely require bathing. They are meticulous groomers and take great pride in their cleanliness. Bathing can often be harmful and stressful for them. It can disrupt the natural oils in their fur and may even lead to hypothermia or shock, especially if not dried properly. Spot cleaning with a damp cloth is usually sufficient for soiled areas.

And there you have it - the magical world of rabbit grooming. By following these steps and showering your rabbit with love and patience, you'll soon become a master at keeping their fur looking fabulous. So grab your brush, gather your courage, and let's hop into the wonderful world of rabbit grooming together!

Chapter 15 - Rabbit Nail & Tooth Care

Rabbits are delightful creatures that bring us endless amounts of joy and laughter. To ensure that our furry friends continue to thrive, it's important to pay close attention to their nails and teeth. These seemingly small body parts are crucial to a rabbit's overall health and well-being. In this chapter, we'll explore the secrets to maintaining your rabbit's nails and teeth, so they can keep hopping, skipping, and jumping with glee!

Maintaining Your Rabbit's Nails

If a rabbit's nails grow too long, it can become painful and difficult for them to hop around. Long nails can also curl under and dig into their paws, causing discomfort and even infection.

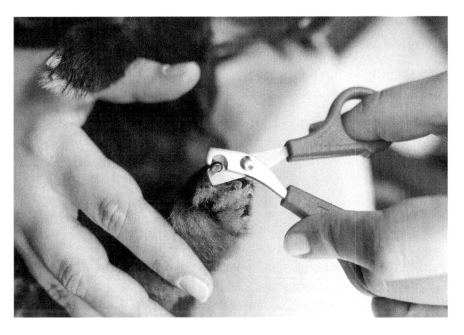

But don't worry, we can help our rabbits by giving them a quick and easy nail trim!

Before we start, it's essential to gather the right tools for the job. A small pair of pet nail clippers or human nail clippers will do the trick. It's also a good idea to have a little cotton ball with some styptic powder or cornstarch nearby, just in case we

accidentally nick the quick (the sensitive part of the nail with blood vessels).

Now, let's get trimming! Gently hold your rabbit's paw and separate one toe at a time. Look for the quick – it's the pinkish area inside the nail. Make sure to only clip the tip of the nail, avoiding the quick, as cutting it can cause pain and bleeding. If you're unsure about how much to trim, start with just a little bit and work your way up.

If you do accidentally nick the quick while trimming your rabbit's nails, don't panic! Apply some styptic powder or cornstarch to a cotton ball and press it gently against the nail to stop any bleeding. It's also a good idea to comfort your rabbit and give them a treat to help them feel better. Remember, accidents happen, but with love, patience, and practice, you'll soon become a nail-trimming pro and keep your rabbit's nails healthy and happy. If the bleeding does not stop or if your furry friend seems to be in a lot of pain, it's important to seek veterinary care as soon as possible. It's always better to be safe than sorry when it comes to our furry friends!

Sometimes, rabbits can be a bit squirmy when it comes to nail trims, so it's essential to be patient and gentle throughout the process. If your rabbit seems too stressed or scared, give them a break and try again later. Remember, practice makes perfect, and soon you and your rabbit will be nail-trimming pros!

Keeping Your Rabbit's Teeth in Tip-Top Shape

Rabbits have big personalities, and their teeth play a starring role in their daily lives. They use their teeth to munch on delicious hay, nibble tasty treats, and explore their surroundings. Unlike humans, rabbit teeth never stop growing, which means it's crucial to keep their chompers in check!

One of the best ways to ensure your rabbit's teeth stay healthy is by providing them with an all-you-can-eat hay buffet. Hay, especially timothy hay, is essential for a rabbit's diet as it helps wear down their teeth and keeps their tummies happy. Place big piles of hay around your rabbit's home for endless snacking opportunities!

In addition to hay, there are plenty of fun toys and chewables that rabbits can nibble on to help maintain their teeth. Wooden toys, cardboard tubes, and apple tree branches are all fantastic options for our furry friends. Not only do these items help keep their teeth in good shape, but they also provide hours of entertainment and mental stimulation.

Of course, sometimes, even with the best care, our rabbits may encounter dental problems. If you notice that your rabbit is having difficulty eating, drooling excessively, or has a change in their droppings, it's essential to visit your trusted veterinarian. They can check your rabbit's teeth and provide the necessary care to keep them munching happily once more.

So, there you have it! Hoppity's secrets to maintaining our rabbits' nails and teeth. By following these tips, we can ensure our fluffy companions stay healthy and content, ready to hop into our hearts for years to come.

Chapter 16 - Common Health Issues

As responsible bunny owners, it's essential to be knowledgeable about the most common health problems that our furry friends may face. From snuffles to sore hocks, from tear duct infections to overgrown teeth, we must understand these issues and how to prevent or treat them.

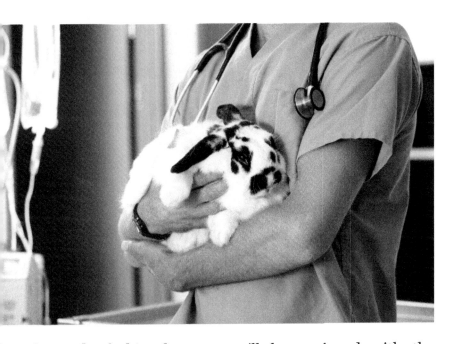

By the end of this chapter, you'll be equipped with the knowledge and tools to keep your rabbit healthy and happy, hopping and binkying to their heart's content.

1. Snuffles: The Sneaky Sneezer

Snuffles is a common health issue among rabbits that can cause discomfort if left untreated. The condition is characterised by sneezing and a runny nose and is caused by a bacterial infection. As a responsible rabbit owner, it's crucial to maintain a clean living environment for your furry friend to prevent the spread of bacteria. If you notice your rabbit exhibiting signs of snuffles, such as persistent sneezing or nasal discharge, it's important to seek veterinary care. With prompt treatment, your bunny can recover quickly and avoid any serious health complications.

2. Tear Duct Infections: The Watery Worry

Tear duct infections in rabbits can cause their eyes to water excessively and become red. If left untreated, these infections can lead to more severe vision problems. To prevent tear duct infections, it's important to keep your rabbit's face clean and free of debris. This can be done by wiping the area gently with a damp cloth. If your rabbit does develop a tear duct infection, it's essential to take them to the vet for treatment. The vet may prescribe medication to help clear up the infection and prevent further damage to your rabbit's eyes. By staying vigilant and keeping your rabbit's face clean, you can help prevent tear duct infections and keep your bunny's eyes healthy and bright.

3. Sore Hocks: The Hurting Hoppers

Sore Hocks, a common condition among rabbits, occurs when the fur on their feet wears away, and the skin underneath becomes red and sore. To avoid this painful condition, rabbits should always have a soft and clean resting place. Regularly cleaning and checking the living area can help keep it clean and prevent the development of sore hocks. In case the condition already developed, a veterinarian can provide special medication to help the rabbits heal. Hoppy and Fluffy wiggled their feet, vowing to take good care of their paws and avoid this unpleasant condition.

4. Overgrown Teeth: The Chewing Challenge

Rabbits have constantly growing teeth, which means that they need to keep them trimmed down by chewing on hard things like hay and vegetables. However, sometimes their teeth can grow too long, making it difficult for them to eat properly. This is called overgrown teeth. To prevent overgrown teeth, it's important to feed your rabbit a balanced diet that includes lots of hay and crunchy vegetables. If your rabbit's teeth do become overgrown, a visit to the vet may be necessary to have them trimmed down. So, make sure your bunny gets plenty of opportunities to chew and gnaw to keep their teeth healthy and strong!

5. Ear Mites: The Itchy Invaders

Ear mites are tiny parasites that can infest a rabbit's ears, causing discomfort and itching. If left untreated, they can lead to more serious ear infections. It's important to keep your rabbit's ears clean and to regularly check for signs of ear mites such as excessive scratching, head shaking, or discharge from the ears. If you suspect your rabbit has ear mites, it's best to consult with a veterinarian who can provide appropriate medication to eliminate the mites and prevent future infestations.

Being a responsible bunny owner requires us to be knowledgeable about the most common health problems that our furry friends may face. From snuffles to sore hocks, from tear duct infections to overgrown teeth and ear mites, we must understand these issues and how to prevent or treat them.

By following the tips and guidelines provided in this chapter, you'll be able to keep your rabbit healthy and happy, free to hop and binky to their heart's content. Always be vigilant and attentive to any signs of discomfort or health issues in your bunny, and don't hesitate to seek veterinary care when needed. With proper care and attention, you can help your furry friend live a long and healthy life full of joy and happiness.

Chapter 17 - Recognising Signs of Illness

Our furry friends can sometimes feel under the weather. It's important for us, as their loving caretakers, to recognise when they're not feeling their best and get them the help they need. This chapter will teach you how to spot signs of illness in your rabbit and when it's time to seek veterinary care.

First, let's get to know our rabbits a little better. Bunnies are experts at hiding their discomfort, as they don't want to show weakness. This is a natural instinct to protect themselves from predators. So, it's essential to keep a close eye on your rabbit and learn to identify subtle changes in their behaviour and appearance.

Signs of Illness

1. Changes in Appetite: A healthy rabbit loves to munch on hay, vegetables, and rabbit pellets. If your bunny isn't eating as much as usual, or if they've stopped eating altogether, it could be a sign that something's wrong. The same goes for their water intake – if they're not drinking enough or drinking too much, it could indicate a health issue.

2. Lethargy: Bunnies are energetic creatures who love to play, hop, and explore. If your rabbit seems to be spending more time than usual lying down or sleeping, it's time to pay attention. Lethargy could be a sign of illness or pain.

3. Changes in Poop: Yes, it's a bit yucky, but keeping an eye on your rabbit's poop is a must! Healthy rabbit poop should

be round, dry, and uniform in size. If you notice their poop is smaller, larger, or a different shape than usual, it could be a sign of trouble. Also, watch out for diarrhoea or if your rabbit stops pooping altogether.

4. Runny Nose or Eyes: If your rabbit has a runny nose or watery eyes, this could indicate a respiratory infection or allergies. Keep an eye out for any discharge or crustiness around their eyes and nose.

5. Fur Loss or Skin Issues: Healthy rabbit fur should be soft, clean, and free of bald patches. If you notice fur loss, redness, or scabs on your rabbit's skin, it's time to investigate further.

6. Trouble Breathing: If your rabbit is breathing faster than usual, panting, or making unusual noises when they breathe, these could be signs of respiratory distress.

7. Changes in Behaviour: As we mentioned earlier, rabbits are experts at hiding their pain. However, they might become more aggressive or less social when they're not feeling well. If your rabbit seems unusually grumpy, scared, or withdrawn, it's essential to take note.

When to Seek Veterinary Care

If you notice any of the signs mentioned above, it's essential to get your rabbit checked out by a veterinarian experienced in treating rabbits. Some illnesses can progress quickly, so it's better to be safe than sorry.

In some cases, your rabbit may need immediate emergency care. If you see any of the following signs, it's time to rush your rabbit to the vet:

1. Seizures or loss of consciousness
2. Severe bleeding
3. Difficulty breathing or gasping for air
4. Inability to move or walk
5. Extreme lethargy or unresponsiveness

Your rabbit relies on you to keep them happy and healthy. By learning to recognise signs of illness and seeking veterinary care when needed, you'll ensure your bunny remains a fluffy, hopping bundle of joy.

Chapter 18 - Keeping Rabbits Healthy and Happy

Once upon a time, in a warm and cozy hutch, there lived two adorable rabbits named Fluffy and Snowball. They were the happiest bunnies in the whole wide world because they had a caring and responsible friend like you! But how did their friend make sure Fluffy and Snowball stayed healthy and happy? Well, they followed some simple preventive care tips and kept up with their vaccinations. Are you ready to learn how to keep your rabbits in tip-top shape? Let's hop right into it!

Preventative Care

Preventive care is super important because it helps your little furry friends stay healthy and avoid any illnesses. Just like us, rabbits need regular check-ups, a good diet, and a clean home. But don't worry, taking care of Fluffy and Snowball isn't hard at all. In fact, it can be a lot of fun!

Regular Check-ups

Rabbit check-ups are just like the ones we have with our doctors. You'll want to take Fluffy and Snowball to see a special rabbit veterinarian, or "rabbit-savvy" vet, at least once a year. The vet will examine your rabbits, check their teeth, listen to their hearts, and look for any signs of illness. You can even make a game out of it by pretending to be a rabbit doctor yourself! Grab a little notebook and write down any questions or concerns you have to share with the vet. Trust me, Fluffy and Snowball will be so grateful that you're looking out for them!

Varied Diet

Now, let's hop over to the topic of diet. Feeding your rabbits the right food is essential to keep them as healthy and strong as superheroes! The most important part of their diet is hay. Hay is like a never-ending bowl of delicious salad, and it's crucial for keeping their teeth and digestive systems in great shape. Your rabbits should always have access to hay, so make sure you fill up their hay rack every day.

Next, you'll want to give them a small amount of fresh vegetables. Vegetables are like the scrumptious dessert after the hay salad. Some rabbit-approved veggies include leafy greens, bell peppers, and herbs. Make sure to wash them well before serving! And remember, just like too much ice cream can give us a tummy ache, too many veggies can upset your rabbit's stomach, so keep the portions small.

Finally, rabbit pellets. Pellets are like the cherry on top of the hay and veggie sundae! They provide extra nutrients for your rabbits, but should only be given in small amounts - around a small handful per day. And don't forget fresh water! Your rabbits should always have access to clean water to quench their thirst after munching on all that tasty food.

Good Hygiene

Now that Fluffy and Snowball have full tummies, it's time to talk about cleanliness. Just like we need a clean room to be comfortable and happy, rabbits need a clean hutch. You should clean their hutch at least once a week by removing any old bedding, wiping down surfaces, and replacing it with fresh bedding. By keeping their home clean, you'll help prevent illnesses and make sure your rabbits are always feeling their best.

Exercise

Bunnies are active creatures, and regular exercise is essential for their physical and mental well-being. Make sure your rabbits have plenty of space to hop and play, or take them for daily supervised playtime in a safe, enclosed area.

Regular grooming is important to prevent fur matting, remove loose fur, and check for any signs of skin issues. You can use a soft brush to gently comb their fur, and a nail clipper to trim their nails when needed.

Parasite Prevention

Parasites are tiny troublemakers that can cause discomfort and make our rabbit friends sick. They come in different forms, like fleas, ticks, and mites, and they can make our furry pals feel itchy and spread diseases. But don't worry, there are ways to protect your rabbits and keep those pesky pests away! Use appropriate parasite prevention products recommended by your vet to keep your rabbits free from these pests.

Environmental Enrichment

Rabbits are intelligent animals and need mental stimulation to prevent boredom and stress. Provide them with toys, tunnels, and other safe objects to explore and play with.

Vaccinations

Last but not least, let's discuss vaccinations. Just like we get vaccines to protect us from diseases, rabbits need vaccinations too! There are two main vaccines that your rabbits should get: one for Myxomatosis and one for Rabbit Hemorrhagic Disease (RHD). These two diseases can be very serious, but the good news is that with the proper vaccinations, Fluffy and Snowball can be protected.

Your rabbit-savvy vet will be able to give your rabbits their vaccinations and guide you on the best schedule for them. It's important to keep track of when your rabbits are due for their vaccines so you can be a responsible rabbit caretaker.

And there you have it! By following these simple preventive care tips and keeping up with vaccinations, you'll be the best friend Fluffy and Snowball could ever ask for. They'll be so proud to have you on their team, working together to keep them healthy and happy. So, grab your rabbit doctor's notebook, and let's get started on this fantastic journey of caring for your adorable rabbits!

Did you know that rabbits can learn tricks and good manners just like your dog or cat? That's right! Rabbits are intelligent and curious animals that can be taught many things using the power of positive reinforcement training. In this chapter, we will explore the world of teaching your fluffy friend new skills and good habits, making your time together even more enjoyable and fun-filled.

First, let's understand what positive reinforcement training means. In simple words, it is a method of teaching animals by rewarding them when they do something right. When your rabbit does something you like, you give them a treat, a gentle pat, or even praise them with kind words. This helps your bunny associate the action with a positive outcome, and they will be more likely to do it again in the future.

Now, let's hop into the world of positive reinforcement training and learn how to teach your rabbit some new tricks and good habits!

1. The Basics: Getting Started

To begin, you will need a few things:

- A quiet, comfortable space for training sessions.
- Small treats that your rabbit loves (like tiny pieces of carrot, apple, or their favourite pellets).
- A clicker (a small device that makes a clicking sound) or a clear, consistent word to use as a marker (like "yes" or "good").
- Patience and a positive attitude.

Before starting a training session, make sure your rabbit is relaxed and comfortable. If they seem stressed or scared, it's best to try another time when they are more at ease.

2. Teaching Your Rabbit to "Target"

One of the first and easiest tricks to teach your rabbit is "targeting." This simply means teaching them to touch their nose to an object (like a small stick or your hand) on command.

Here's how you do it:

- Hold the target (a small stick or your hand) close to your rabbit's nose. As soon as they sniff or touch it, give them a treat and use your clicker or say your marker word.
- Repeat this process several times, gradually increasing the distance between the target and your rabbit's nose. Always reward them when they touch the target.
- Once your rabbit is consistently touching the target, you can add a cue word, like "touch" or "target." Say the cue word just before they touch the target, and soon they will understand the connection between the word and the action.

3. Teaching Your Rabbit to "Come"

Wouldn't it be wonderful if your rabbit came hopping to you every time you called their name? Here's how you can teach them to do just that:

- Start by sitting close to your rabbit and calling their name. If they even slightly move towards you, use your clicker or marker word and give them a treat.
- Gradually increase the distance between you and your rabbit, rewarding them each time they come closer to you when called.
- Eventually, your rabbit will learn to associate their name with coming to you and getting a treat. Remember to always reward them for coming, even if it takes them a while!

This adorable trick has your rabbit sitting up on their hind legs, looking like a cute, furry little person. Here's how to teach your rabbit to "sit up":

- Hold a treat above your rabbit's head, just out of their reach. They will naturally stretch up to try and get it.
- As soon as your rabbit sits up on their hind legs, use your clicker or marker word and give them the treat.
- Repeat this process until your rabbit consistently sits up when you hold a treat above their head. Then, add a cue word like "sit up" or "up" just before they perform the action.
- Remember, patience is key! It may take some time for your rabbit to learn this trick, but with consistent practice, they'll get there.

5.   Good Habits: Litter Training

Positive reinforcement training can also be used to teach your rabbit good habits, like using a litter box. Here's how:

- Observe your rabbit and notice where they naturally like to go to the bathroom. Place a litter box in that area.
- Whenever you see your rabbit using the litter box, reward them with a treat and use your clicker or marker word.
- If you catch your rabbit going to the bathroom outside the litter box, gently place them in the box and reward them when they use it.

- Be patient and consistent. It may take some time, but your rabbit will eventually learn to use the litter box.

With a little patience, love, and positive reinforcement, you'll be amazed at what your rabbit can learn. The bond between you and your furry friend will grow stronger as you work together, making your life together happier and more harmonious.

Remember, every rabbit is unique, and they will learn at their own pace. Be patient with your bunny and celebrate their progress, no matter how small. After all, the journey of learning together is just as important as the destination. Happy training!

Chapter 20 - Tricks and Games

Do you want to have a fantastic time with your rabbit while teaching them cool tricks and playing fun games? Well, get ready to embark on an exciting adventure into the world of rabbit tricks and games! In this chapter, we'll explore a variety of tricks and games that you can enjoy with your furry friend.

Tricks

Let's start with tricks! Rabbits are intelligent animals and can learn some impressive tricks with a little patience and practice.

Spinning in a Circle

One simple trick you can teach your rabbit is spinning in a circle. Hold a treat and guide your rabbit in a circular motion, rewarding them with the treat each time they complete the circle. With practice, your rabbit will spin like a pro!

Hurdles!

Another trick you can try is teaching your rabbit to jump over a small obstacle. Set up a low hurdle using books or other safe objects and encourage your rabbit to hop over it with a treat or their favourite toy as motivation. With determination and practice, your rabbit will impress you with their jumping skills!

Fetch

Yes, rabbits can learn to retrieve objects too! Start by using a small toy or ball that your rabbit can hold in their mouth. Encourage them to pick up the toy by placing it near their mouth and rewarding them when they touch it. Gradually increase the distance they need to move to reach the toy and reward them for bringing it back to you

High Five

Teach your rabbit to give you a high five with their paw. Start by gently touching their paw and rewarding them with a treat. Gradually raise your hand higher, encouraging them to lift their

paw to meet your hand. When they successfully touch your hand, give them a treat and praise them.

Play Dead

This trick involves teaching your rabbit to lie down and play dead on command. Start by gently guiding them into a lying position, rewarding them with a treat and verbal praise. As they become more comfortable with the position, introduce a verbal cue such as "play dead" or "rest" while guiding them. Reward them generously when they respond to the cue.

Games

Now, let's dive into games! Rabbits love to play and spend time with their owners, playing games with them will keep them happy and entertained.

Treat Hunt

One fun game you can play with your rabbit is the "Treat Hunt." Hide small treats around a designated area and encourage your rabbit to sniff them out and find them. This game taps into their natural foraging instincts and keeps them engaged and entertained.

Guessing Game

You can also stimulate your rabbit's senses with the "Scent Guessing Game." Hide different scents, such as herbs or fruits, under cups or in boxes and let your rabbit use their keen sense of smell to find the hidden scent. They'll have a wonderful time sniffing and searching for their favourite scent and you'll get to learn about their favourite things.

Tunnel Dash

Another game you can try is the "Tunnel Dash." Set up tunnels or create obstacle courses using boxes, tubes, or other safe materials. Encourage your rabbit to explore, hop through tunnels, and navigate the course. It's a great way for them to exercise and have a blast!

Bunny Bowling

Create your own bowling game using safe, lightweight pins and a soft ball. Set up the pins and encourage your rabbit to nudge the ball and knock them down. It's a playful and entertaining game that allows your rabbit to showcase their agility and coordination.

Remember, every rabbit is unique, so be patient and adapt the tricks and games to their individual abilities and preferences. Always provide a safe and supervised environment during playtime to ensure their well-being.

By teaching your rabbit tricks and playing games together, you'll strengthen the bond between you and create lasting memories. The joy and laughter you share will brighten both of your days. So, get ready for a world of excitement and fun with your amazing rabbit companion!

Chapter 21 - Building a Strong Bond

Building a strong bond with your furry friend is a wonderful and rewarding experience. Just like any friendship, the bond between a rabbit and their human is built on love, trust, and understanding. In this chapter, we will explore the key steps to foster a strong bond with your rabbit companion.

Create a Comforting Environment

Providing a cozy and comfortable living space is crucial for your rabbit's well-being and the bond you share. Ensure they have a clean and comfortable area with soft bedding, fresh water, and nutritious food.

Rabbits are naturally curious and need a stimulating environment, so add toys and hiding spots to create an enriching space. Rotating toys and introducing new ones from time to time can keep things interesting.

Additionally, provide opportunities for exercise and exploration, such as supervised time outside of their enclosure or designated play areas within your home. A secure and welcoming space will help your rabbit feel safe and loved, fostering a stronger bond between you.

Gentle Communication

Communication is essential in any relationship, and it plays a crucial role in bonding with your rabbit. While rabbits may not understand human language, they can sense your tone and intentions.

- Speak softly and kindly to your rabbit, using positive words to make them feel safe and loved.

- Use gentle touches and strokes to show your affection.

- Take the time to observe your rabbit's body language and respond accordingly.

Each rabbit has unique preferences and comfort levels, so it's important to pay attention and respect their boundaries. The more you communicate in a gentle and understanding manner, the stronger your bond will become.

Play and Have Fun

Engaging in playtime activities with your rabbit is not only enjoyable but also a fantastic way to strengthen your bond.

Discover what games and toys your rabbit enjoys and make time for regular play sessions. This could include activities like hopping through obstacle courses, playing with toys, or even engaging in gentle chasing games.

Each rabbit has unique preferences, so try different activities to see what brings them joy. Remember to create a safe environment and supervise playtime to prevent accidents. Through play, you'll not only provide mental and physical stimulation for your rabbit but also deepen your bond and create cherished memories together.

Rabbits have unique personalities, and understanding their feelings and needs is essential in building a strong bond.

Pay close attention to their body language, behaviours, and preferences. Notice how they respond to different situations and environments. Rabbits communicate through various cues, such as ear position, body posture, and vocalisations.

By learning to interpret your rabbit's signals, you can better understand their emotions and needs. This understanding allows you to provide the care and support they require, deepening the connection between you and your furry friend.

Patience and Consistency

Building a strong bond with your rabbit takes time and patience. Each rabbit is an individual with their own background and experiences.

- Be patient and allow your rabbit to adjust to their new environment and form trust at their own pace.

- Be consistent in your interactions and daily routines.

- Establish trust by being reliable and predictable.

- Provide regular feeding times, play sessions, and grooming sessions.

- Avoid sudden changes or disruptions to their routines as it can cause stress.

With patience and consistency, your bond will grow stronger over time, and your rabbit will learn to trust and rely on you as their companion.

Remember, each rabbit is unique, and the bond you form will be a special connection between you and your furry friend. Cherish the moments you share, and embrace the joy and love that come with a strong rabbit-human bond. Through gentle communication, a comforting environment, shared playtime, understanding their needs, and practicing patience and consistency, you can cultivate a bond that will bring you and your rabbit happiness and fulfilment for years to

Introducing rabbits to one another or integrating them with other pets in your household can be an exciting but delicate process. With careful planning, patience, and guidance, you can create a harmonious environment where all your furry friends can coexist happily. In this chapter, we will explore the steps and considerations involved in introducing new rabbits to an existing rabbit or integrating rabbits with other pets.

Preparing for Introduction

Before initiating any introductions, it's important to ensure that you have the necessary preparations in place. This section will guide you through the essential steps to create a safe and comfortable environment for your rabbits and other pets.

Assessing Compatibility: Understanding Your Pets

Before introducing rabbits, it's crucial to assess the temperament, behaviour, and social needs of both your existing rabbit and the newcomer. Consider factors such as age, sex, and personality traits. Some rabbits may be more sociable and accepting of new companions, while others may be more territorial or independent.

Veterinary Check-up: Ensuring Health and Safety

Schedule a visit to the veterinarian to ensure that all your pets are healthy and up to date on vaccinations. This is particularly important when introducing rabbits to other pets, as it helps minimise the risk of potential diseases or infections.

Separate Living Spaces

Create separate living spaces for your existing rabbit and the newcomer, each with their own enclosure, food, water, and litter box. This allows them to become familiar with their individual territories and ensures their safety during the introduction process.

Gradual Introduction Techniques

Introducing rabbits gradually and in a controlled manner is essential to minimise stress and potential conflicts. This section will provide step-by-step guidance on different introduction techniques.

Start by introducing the rabbits to each other's scents. Swap bedding or toys between their enclosures, allowing them to become familiar with each other's scent without direct contact. This helps establish a sense of familiarity and reduces anxiety during subsequent face-to-face introductions.

Neutral Territory: A Safe Meeting Ground

Choose a neutral space, such as a large playpen or a neutral room, for the initial face-to-face introductions. This neutral territory reduces the chances of territorial disputes and allows the rabbits to interact on neutral ground.

Supervised Interaction: Slow and Steady

During the initial meetings, closely supervise the rabbits' interactions. Keep a close eye on their body language, ensuring that they exhibit signs of curiosity and relaxation rather than aggression or fear. If any signs of tension arise, separate them and try again later.

Short and Positive Encounters

Begin with short, positive encounters between the rabbits, gradually increasing the duration as they become more comfortable with each other. Offer treats and praise to reinforce positive behaviours and associations during these interactions.

Introducing Rabbits to Other Pets

Integrating rabbits with other pets, such as dogs or cats, requires careful introductions to ensure the safety and well-being of all animals involved. This section will provide guidance on introducing rabbits to other pets in your household.

Assessing Compatibility

Evaluate the temperament, energy levels, and previous experiences of your other pets. Consider their prey drive, predatory instincts, and history of interactions with small animals. Not all pets may be suitable for cohabitation with rabbits, and the safety of all animals should be the top priority.

Controlled Interactions: Safety First

Initially, introduce the rabbits and other pets through barriers or gates, allowing them to see and smell each other without direct physical contact. This controlled interaction allows them to become familiar with each other's presence while maintaining a safe distance.

Gradual Exposure: Controlled Encounters

Gradually increase the exposure between the rabbits and other pets by allowing supervised, controlled encounters in a neutral area. Use leashes or harnesses for dogs, and keep cats on a leash or in a carrier. Monitor their reactions closely and intervene if any signs of aggression or distress arise.

Rewarding Good Behaviour

Reward positive behaviour and calm interactions between the rabbits and other pets with treats, praise, and gentle petting. Create positive associations by providing treats and attention to both parties when they display friendly behaviour towards each other.

Separate Spaces: Ensuring Safety

Maintain separate living spaces for the rabbits and other pets, especially when unsupervised. This ensures that each animal has a safe retreat and reduces the risk of potential conflicts or accidents.

Patience and Monitoring

Introducing rabbits to an existing rabbit or other pets requires patience and ongoing monitoring. This section emphasises the importance of patience and vigilance throughout the integration process.

Time and Patience: Allowing for Adjustment

Recognise that each animal may require a different amount of time to adjust to the presence of others. Avoid rushing the process and be patient with their individual comfort levels and progress.

Monitoring and Intervention: Ensuring Safety

Continuously monitor the interactions between the rabbits and other pets, especially during the initial stages of integration. Be prepared to intervene if any signs of aggression or distress occur, and separate the animals if necessary.

Seeking Help if Needed

If you encounter significant challenges or concerns during the introduction process, seek guidance from a professional animal behaviourist or veterinarian experienced in multi-pet dynamics. They can provide valuable insights and tailored advice to address specific issues.

Introducing rabbits to an existing rabbit or other pets in your household requires careful planning, patience, and ongoing monitoring. By following the steps outlined in this chapter and providing a safe and controlled environment, you can foster a harmonious relationship between your furry friends. Remember, every animal is unique, and the integration process may vary. With time, understanding, and positive reinforcement, you can build a loving and cohesive multi-pet household where rabbits and other pets can thrive together.

Chapter 23 - The History of Rabbits

Today, we love these little creatures and enjoy their company as pets, but have you ever wondered about their incredible journey through history? Let's hop back in time and explore the fascinating story of rabbits!

Long, long ago, rabbits first roamed the Earth around 40 million years ago. They lived in the vast lands of North America and Europe, where they had lots of space to roam free and munch on their favourite green plants. Back then, rabbits were wild, and they had to be clever and quick to avoid predators like birds, foxes, and other animals that wanted to eat them for dinner!

As time went by, rabbits continued to evolve and adapt to their environment. Around 4000 BC, people started to notice these cute, little creatures hopping around the European continent. Can you imagine being the first person to see a rabbit? Your eyes would widen with amazement and your heart would fill with joy!

During the Roman Empire, around 200 BC, rabbits began to become more than just wild animals. People started to capture them and keep them in enclosures called 'leporaria.' The Romans saw these furry animals as a source of food and fur, but they also discovered how intelligent and endearing rabbits could be.

Rabbits soon spread across Europe, and by the Middle Ages, they had become a popular animal to keep in manors and castles. Kings, queens, and nobles began to raise rabbits for their meat and fur, but they also found joy in watching them hop and play. It was during this time that domestication of rabbits truly began. People started to breed rabbits with different colours and patterns, creating a beautiful array of bunnies that we see today.

In the 1700s and 1800s, rabbit-keeping became a popular hobby for people of all ages, and rabbit shows began popping up where proud owners displayed their prized bunnies. It was an exciting time for rabbit enthusiasts, as they could show off their fluffy friends and admire the unique qualities of each rabbit. Can you imagine the feeling of pride they had when their beloved bunny won a prize?

During the 19th century, rabbits hopped their way across the ocean and arrived in Australia. People brought them there to hunt for sport, but little did they know, these rabbits had other plans! They reproduced so quickly that Australia soon had a rabbit population of over 10 million! The country was overrun with rabbits, and they became a significant problem for the environment and agriculture. It was a lesson for humans to be careful when introducing animals to new habitats.

Meanwhile, in the United States, a man named George S. West wanted to create the perfect rabbit breed. In the 1920s, he began to work on a new breed called the Californian rabbit. This rabbit was a blend of different breeds, and it had beautiful white fur with dark markings on its ears, nose, feet, and tail. Wests' dream came true, and Californian rabbits became popular all over the world!

As the years passed, people continued to fall in love with rabbits, and they began to keep them as pets in their homes. They discovered that rabbits were not only cute but also smart, loving, and full of personality. Families started to adopt rabbits and welcome them into their homes, where they found joy and companionship from these gentle creatures.

Today, there are over 300 different rabbit breeds, each with its unique features and characteristics. We have rabbits with long, floppy ears, rabbits with short, round bodies, and even rabbits with curly, wavy fur! There are so many rabbits to love and cherish, and our history with these wonderful creatures continues to grow.

As you can see, rabbits have had an incredible journey throughout history. They have hopped their way from wild animals to the loving pets we know today. So, the next time you see a rabbit, remember its fascinating story and appreciate how far it has come. Rabbits truly have a special place in our hearts and history, and they will continue to bring joy and happiness to people all around the world.

Chapter 24 - Fascinating Facts and Trivia

These fluffy, lovable creatures have been our companions for centuries, and they continue to bring joy and excitement to people of all ages. Our fluffy, furry friends are incredibly special, as they possess some truly unique characteristics and abilities that set them apart from other animals. In this chapter, we'll take you on a journey through the most fascinating facts and trivia about rabbits. Are you ready to explore the rabbit hole? Let's dive in!

The Secret Language of Rabbits

Rabbits may not have the gift of speech like humans, but they have their unique way of communicating, using a secret language that is both mysterious and enchanting. Rabbits express their feelings and emotions through a series of body language signals, which can be quite fascinating to observe.

For example, when a rabbit is happy and relaxed, it may stretch out and lie down with its legs tucked under its body, resembling a soft and fluffy loaf of bread. On the other hand, when a rabbit is frightened or anxious, it may thump its powerful hind legs on the ground, sending a warning signal to its fellow rabbits.

Another endearing aspect of rabbit communication is the "binky," a delightful expression of joy and happiness. When a rabbit performs a binky, it leaps into the air, twisting and turning its body with sheer excitement. Witnessing a binky is a heartwarming experience, reminding us of the simple joys and pleasures that life has to offer.

The Art of Digging

Rabbits are naturally gifted in the art of digging, using their strong and sturdy legs to create intricate burrows and tunnels. In the wild, rabbits use their exceptional digging skills to construct elaborate underground homes known as "warrens." These warrens can be quite extensive, housing entire rabbit families and providing them with a safe and cozy refuge from the outside world.

Although domestic rabbits may not have the need to dig a warren, their innate love for digging remains strong. Providing your rabbit with a designated digging area, such as a sandbox or a digging box filled with child-safe play sand, can help satisfy their natural instincts and keep them happy and content.

Amazing Rabbit Ears

First and foremost, one cannot help but notice the rabbits' most iconic feature - their long and pointy ears. But did you know that these remarkable ears are not just for show? They serve a vital purpose, making rabbits one of the best listeners in the animal kingdom!

A rabbit's ears can grow up to 4 inches long, and they are packed with a vast network of blood vessels and nerve endings. This enables them to detect even the faintest of sounds from miles away. With their remarkable hearing, rabbits can quickly identify potential threats or predators and sprint away in a flash, leaving their pursuers in the dust!

Moreover, rabbit ears are incredibly flexible, allowing them to swivel almost 270 degrees, like a high-tech radar dish. This amazing ability helps rabbits stay alert and aware of their surroundings at all times, ensuring their safety and well-being.

Rabbit ears also help regulate body temperature. When it's hot outside, rabbits can cool down by circulating blood through their large, thin ears. In the cold, they can keep their ears close to their body to conserve heat. How cool is that?

Super Scent

A rabbit's nose is nothing short of a superhero feature! Their small, twitchy noses possess an astonishing 100 million scent receptors. To put that into perspective, humans have a mere 6 million scent receptors in comparison. This means that rabbits have an extraordinary sense of smell, which is critical for their survival.

Thanks to their super-powered noses, rabbits can easily sniff out their favourite foods, detect hidden dangers, and even dentify their friends and family members. It's no wonder that these fluffy creatures are often seen twitching their noses, as

they constantly gather vital information from their environment.

The Rabbit's Incredible Speed

Rabbits are known for their incredible speed and agility, which is crucial for their survival in the wild. With their powerful hind legs, these amazing creatures can leap up to 4 feet high and 9 feet long in a single bound! Moreover, rabbits can reach speeds of up to 30 miles per hour, making them one of the fastest animals on the planet.

Their remarkable agility, combined with their exceptional hearing and sense of smell, makes rabbits true masters of escape. Predators may try their luck, but catching a rabbit is no easy feat!

A Bunny is Not Just a Bunny

Did you know that there are more than 300 different breeds of rabbits in the world? Wow! That's a lot of bunny variety! Some of the most popular breeds include the Holland Lop, the Netherland Dwarf, and the Flemish Giant. Each breed has its unique physical characteristics, personality traits, and care requirements. So, whether you prefer a tiny, adorable ball of fluff or a gentle, massive bunny, there's a perfect rabbit for everyone!

A Toothsome Fact

Rabbit teeth never stop growing! That's right, their teeth continuously grow throughout their lives, at a rate of about 3 millimetres (0.12 inches) per month. To keep their teeth at a manageable length, rabbits need to constantly chew on hay, wooden toys, and other materials. So, if you ever see a rabbit chewing away, just remember that they're doing it for a good reason.

The Rabbit's Digestive System

Rabbits have a unique and complex digestive system. They are herbivores, meaning they only eat plant material. However, they also have a special way of processing their food called "hindgut fermentation." This process involves the rabbit eating its own droppings, known as cecotropes, to absorb more nutrients from its food. While it might sound strange to us, it's completely normal and essential for rabbits to maintain a healthy digestive system.

Rabbits in Popular Culture

Rabbits have been a part of our stories and folklore for centuries. Rabbits in popular fiction, TV, and movies have captured our hearts and imaginations. Even today, rabbits continue to be a popular choice for characters in books, movies, and television shows, enchanting audiences of all ages.

In many cultures, rabbits have been a symbol of fertility, rebirth, and good luck. For example, in ancient Egypt, rabbits were associated with the moon and were believed to have the power to bring forth new life. Similarly, in European folklore, the "Easter Bunny" delivers eggs to children, symbolising the renewal of life during springtime.

In conclusion, rabbits are truly extraordinary creatures, possessing a unique set of characteristics and abilities that make them stand out in the animal kingdom. These enchanting and endearing qualities have captured the hearts and imaginations of people around the world, making rabbits one of the most beloved and cherished pets. So, the next time you see a rabbit, take a moment to appreciate the magic and wonder that these remarkable animals bring to our lives.

Chapter 25 - DIY Rabbit Toys and Accessories

In this chapter, we're going to explore the fantastic world of DIY rabbit toys and accessories. These incredible creations will not only make your furry friends jump for joy, but they'll also keep their minds and bodies healthy and active. So, let's hop right into it and discover how you can become a master of DIY rabbit toys and accessories!

The world of rabbits is full of excitement and curiosity. They love exploring and playing with anything they can find. However, it's important to provide them with safe and engaging toys that will stimulate their minds and satisfy their natural instincts. With just a little bit of creativity and some simple materials, you can create magical toys and accessories that your rabbits will adore.

Toys

To begin our journey, let's start with some easy-to-make toys that will keep your bunnies entertained for hours:

Rabbits love to have their very own kingdom to rule! With a few cardboard boxes, scissors, and non-toxic glue, you can create a marvellous castle for your furry royals. Cut out doorways and windows for your rabbits to hop through, and add some tunnels and ramps for extra adventure. This majestic cardboard castle will give your bunnies a place to play, hide, and explore.

2.   The Tasty Treat Ball

A treat ball is a tasty toy that rewards your rabbits with a delicious surprise. All you need is a small, rabbit-safe plastic ball with holes and some of their favourite treats. Fill the ball with the treats, and watch your rabbits roll it around and nibble at the yummy treasures inside. This entertaining treat ball not only provides fun and tasty rewards but also encourages exercise and mental stimulation.

3.   The Whimsical Willow Wreath

Rabbits love to chew on things, and a willow wreath is the perfect toy to satisfy their nibbling needs. Simply weave fresh, untreated willow branches into a circle, and let your rabbits have a munching good time. Chewing on the whimsical willow wreath not only keeps your bunnies entertained, but it also helps to maintain their dental health.

Living Space Accessories

Now that we've explored rabbit toys, let's hop on over to the world of delightful accessories. These enchanting creations will not only make your rabbits' living space more comfortable, but they'll also add a touch of charm and warmth:

1.   Cuddle Cup

A cuddle cup is a soft and snug place where your rabbits can curl up and relax. To make this cozy accessory, you'll need some fleece fabric, a sewing machine or needle and thread, and some soft stuffing. Cut two circles of fleece, sew them together, and stuff them with the filling. This fluffy cuddle cup will provide your bunnies with a warm and inviting place to snuggle.

A hay feeder is an essential accessory that helps to keep your rabbits' hay clean and organised. With a wire storage rack or a simple wooden frame, you can create a hay feeder that will enchant your bunnies. Attach the rack or frame to the side of your rabbits' enclosure and fill it with fresh hay. This hay feeder not only keeps the hay tidy but also makes it easier for your rabbits to munch on their favourite food.

As we come to the end of our journey through the magical world of DIY rabbit toys and accessories, remember that the most important ingredient in creating these items is your love and care for your furry friends. By crafting these wonderful toys and accessories, you're not only making your rabbits happy, but you're also strengthening the bond between you and your beloved pets.

So, gather your materials, put on your creative hat, and embark on the exciting adventure of making your own rabbit toys and accessories. Your bunnies will be forever grateful, and your heart will be filled with the joy of knowing that you've made their lives more fun, and comfortable. Happy crafting!

Chapter 26 - DIY Rabbit-Friendly Treats

Are you ready to get your chef hat on and prepare some scrumptious, rabbit-friendly treats? Let's hop right into the kitchen and start creating delectable delights for our fluffy bunny friends! As you may know, rabbits have a pretty basic diet of hay, fresh vegetables, and some pellets. But every now and then, wouldn't it be fun to surprise them with a tasty treat that they'll absolutely love?

In this chapter, we will be exploring some super easy and exciting recipes that are not only delicious but also provide our bunnies with essential nutrients. Plus, you'll be able to proudly say that you made these treats yourself!

But before we get started, remember that treats should always be given in moderation. It's like when you're allowed to enjoy a tiny piece of cake at a birthday party, but having too much might make you feel sick. The same goes for our rabbit friends; they can have a little bit of fun, but we don't want them to get tummy troubles!

Now, let's get cooking!

Fruity Ice Pops

Ingredients:

- **1 apple**

- **1 banana**

- **A handful of fresh berries (blueberries, raspberries, or strawberries)**

- **A few fresh mint leaves**

Instructions:

1. Begin by washing the apple and berries. You can ask an adult to help you cut the apple into small pieces, removing the seeds and core.

2. Peel the banana and slice it into small circles.

3. In a large bowl, gently mix the apple pieces, banana slices, and berries. Be careful not to squish the fruits!

4. Fill an ice cube tray with the mixture, pressing the fruit down to make sure there's no empty space.

5. Add a tiny mint leaf to each ice cube compartment for an extra touch of freshness.

6. Pop the ice cube tray in the freezer and wait for a few hours until the fruity ice pops are completely frozen.

7. Once frozen, take them out and give your rabbit an icy treat on a warm day. They will love nibbling on this chilly, fruity surprise!

Veggie Delight Bites

Ingredients:

- **1 small sweet potato**
- **2 medium-sized carrots**
- **A handful of kale leaves, chopped**
- **A pinch of dried rose petals (optional)**

Instructions:

1. Preheat your oven to 350°F (180°C) and line a baking sheet with parchment paper.

2. Wash the sweet potato and carrots. You can ask an adult to help you peel and grate them into thin shreds.

3. In a large mixing bowl, combine the grated sweet potato, grated carrots, and chopped kale.

4. Scoop out small spoonfuls of the mixture and shape them into bite-sized balls. Place each ball onto the prepared baking sheet.

5. If you have dried rose petals, sprinkle a few on top of each veggie delight bite for a beautiful and fragrant touch.

6. Bake the veggie bites in the oven for about 25-30 minutes until they are firm and slightly golden.

7. Allow them to cool completely before treating your rabbit to these yummy, nutritious nibbles!

Bunny Banana Pancakes

Ingredients:

- **1 ripe banana**

- **1 cup of rolled oats**

- **1 cup of water**

- **A small handful of fresh parsley, chopped**

Instructions:

1. In a blender or food processor, combine the rolled oats and water. Blend until you have a smooth, pancake-like batter.

2. Mash the ripe banana in a bowl with a fork, then add it to the oat batter. Mix well.

3. Stir in the chopped parsley, making sure it's evenly distributed throughout the batter.

4. Preheat a non-stick pan over low heat. You can ask an adult to help you with this part.

5. Pour small spoonfuls of batter onto the pan, making mini pancakes. Cook them for about 2-3 minutes on each side, until they're golden brown.

6. Allow the bunny banana pancakes to cool before serving them to your rabbit. Watch as they enjoy this special breakfast treat!

Remember, these treats are meant to be given in small amounts as an occasional surprise for your bunny. Be sure to store any leftovers in the fridge or freezer and use them within a week.

We hope you and your rabbit enjoy these delightful, homemade treats. It's always a joy to see our furry friends happily nibbling on something we've made with love. So put on your apron, gather your ingredients, and let's make our rabbits the happiest bunnies around!

Chapter 27 - Wild Rabbits

Have you ever wondered how rabbits live in the wild? These cute and fluffy animals are fascinating creatures, and they have a lot more to them than meets the eye. So, hop along with me on this exciting adventure as we explore the natural habitats, food, and lifestyle of wild rabbits!

Home Sweet Home

Wild rabbits can be found all over the world, from the snowy regions of the Arctic to the hot deserts of Africa. However, most rabbits prefer to live in grassy fields, meadows, and woodlands, where there's plenty of food and shelter. Just like humans, rabbits need a comfortable and safe home, and they're experts at finding the perfect spot!

In these areas, rabbits live in complex burrow systems called 'warrens.' Warrens are like a rabbit's mansion, with multiple rooms and entrances. They dig these tunnels and chambers themselves, using their powerful hind legs and sharp claws. Imagine being able to build your own house with just your legs and nails!

Warrens are not just a place for rabbits to sleep, but they also serve as a hiding place from predators, like foxes, badgers, and birds of prey. Rabbits are pretty clever, huh? They create multiple escape routes in their warrens, so if danger comes knocking, they can make a quick getaway!

The Rabbit Foodie

Now that we know where rabbits live, let's talk about what they eat! Rabbits are herbivores, which means they only eat plants. In the wild, their diet consists of grass, leaves, flowers, and even tree bark. These plant-based foods provide rabbits with all the essential nutrients they need to stay healthy and strong.

Rabbits have a unique way of eating, too! They are 'crepuscular,' which means they're most active during the early mornings and late evenings. This is the perfect time for them to munch on plants because it's cooler, and there are fewer predators lurking around. So, while you're enjoying your breakfast or dinner, rabbits are feasting on their favourite greens as well!

Moreover, rabbits have an incredible digestive system that helps them break down all that plant material. They even practice something called 'coprophagy,' which means they eat their own poop! I know it sounds gross, but this actually helps them absorb more nutrients from their food. So, next time you see a rabbit nibbling on something, don't be too quick to judge!

The Social Life of Rabbits

Rabbits are not only adorable and fluffy but also sociable creatures. They live together in groups called 'colonies,' and they rely on each other for companionship, protection, and the occasional grooming session. Rabbits are very affectionate with each other, and they love to cuddle up with their buddies for warmth and comfort. It's like having a sleepover with your best friends every single night!

Within a colony, there's a social hierarchy, with one dominant male, also known as the 'alpha,' who's in charge. The alpha rabbit gets first dibs on the best food and the cosiest spots in the warren. But don't worry, the other rabbits in the colony still have each other's backs, and they work together to ensure everyone's safety and well-being.

The Language of Rabbits

Did you know that rabbits have their own way of communicating? They use body language, sounds, and even scent to express themselves. For example, when a rabbit is happy or excited, it might do a little dance called a 'binky,' where it hops and twists in the air. It's like they're saying, "I'm so happy, I just can't contain myself!"

Rabbits also thump their hind legs on the ground to warn other rabbits of danger. This loud noise alerts the whole colony, so they can all run to safety. It's like having a personal alarm system that's always on the lookout for danger!

Lastly, rabbits use scent glands under their chin to mark their territory or show affection. They rub their chin on objects, other rabbits, or even you to say, "This is mine," or "I like you!"

In the wild, rabbits have a tough life, and they face many challenges. They have to constantly watch out for predators, find food, and deal with harsh weather conditions. Because of these challenges, rabbits have a shorter lifespan in the wild, usually around 1-2 years.

However, rabbits are also incredible survivors. They can adapt to different environments, and they reproduce quickly to ensure their species continues to thrive. Female rabbits, called 'does,' can give birth to multiple litters of babies, known as 'kits,' throughout the year. This means that even though life in the wild can be tough, rabbits always find a way to bounce back!

In conclusion, the world of wild rabbits is truly amazing. From their cozy burrows to their unique eating habits, these remarkable creatures show us that there's always more to learn about the animal kingdom. So, the next time you spot a rabbit hopping in the wild, take a moment to appreciate the incredible journey they go through every day, and remember that we share this beautiful planet with countless other wonderful creatures.

Rabbits are incredible creatures that have adapted to various environments across the world. From forests to deserts, cities to mountains, they showcase remarkable resilience and resourcefulness. In this chapter, we will explore how rabbits adapt to different environments and thrive in diverse landscapes.

Forest Dwellers

In lush green forests, rabbits have evolved specific traits to navigate their habitat successfully. They possess large, powerful hind legs, enabling them to leap over fallen logs and climb steep hills. Their thick fur acts as camouflage, helping them blend seamlessly into the environment and avoid predators. Forest rabbits have learned to nibble on tree barks, search for tender leaves and grasses, and escape danger by leaping into the air and disappearing into dense foliage. These adaptations allow them to thrive and survive in the forest's challenging conditions.

Desert rabbits face an entirely different set of challenges. To adapt to arid landscapes with scorching temperatures, they have developed unique characteristics. Their large ears play a crucial role in regulating body temperature, dissipating heat and keeping them cool. Long, strong legs enable them to run swiftly and escape from predators. Desert rabbits have also mastered the art of burrow digging, creating deep shelters to escape the intense heat during the day. At night, they emerge to forage for food and obtain moisture from the plants they eat, such as cacti. These adaptations enable desert rabbits to survive and thrive in seemingly inhospitable desert environments.

Thriving in the Urban Jungle

Cities may seem like an unlikely place for rabbits, but they have proven their adaptability even in bustling urban environments. City rabbits have honed their senses to navigate the concrete jungles with agility and find shelter in parks and gardens. They possess keen awareness of their surroundings, always staying alert to avoid potential dangers. These resourceful rabbits have earned to forage for food within the city limits, munching on grasses, flowers, and even vegetables from urban gardens. Their bravery and adaptability in making a home in the unfamiliar urban environment are truly impressive.

Conquering the Mountains

The snowy mountain ranges pose yet another set of challenges for rabbits. To survive in the cold and snowy conditions, mountain rabbits have evolved distinct adaptations. Their thick fur, often white in colour, serves as insulation against the frigid temperatures and helps them blend into the snow-covered landscape, providing camouflage from predators. Mountain rabbits also possess powerful legs, allowing them to move effortlessly through deep snow. Their strong, sharp claws aid in digging into the icy ground to find food. These adaptations enable them to thrive in the harsh mountain environment.

Through these examples, we witness the incredible adaptability of rabbits to different environments. Each habitat presents its own challenges, and rabbits have developed unique physical traits and behaviours to overcome them. Their ability to thrive in diverse landscapes is a testament to their resilience and resourcefulness.

As we explore the world of rabbits and their remarkable adaptations, we gain a deeper appreciation for these creatures. Whether it be forests, deserts, cities, or mountains, rabbits have proven time and again that they can not only survive but thrive in diverse environments. Their adaptability and curiosity are qualities that continue to inspire us as we appreciate the wonders of the natural world.

Rabbits are enchanting creatures that can bring immense happiness into our lives. They are gentle, loving, and have unique personalities that make them delightful companions.

Just imagine sitting in a cozy corner while your fluffy little rabbit snuggles up beside you, their soft fur brushing against your skin, and their tiny heart beating in rhythm with yours. It's a magical moment that brings a sense of serenity and warmth, making you feel loved and connected.

The first time you lay your eyes on a rabbit, it's easy to fall in love with their soft, velvety fur, and their adorably twitching noses. Their large, inquisitive eyes seem to hold a world of secrets, and their long, floppy ears sway gracefully with each hop, as if dancing to the melody of life. Their cute, cotton-tail bounces behind them, leaving a trail of joy and happiness wherever they go.

Rabbits are also remarkably social creatures, forming strong bonds with their fellow bunnies and their human caretakers. They love to play, explore, and cuddle with their favourite humans, often following them around the house like a shadow. When you come home after a long, tiring day, there's nothing quite like the sight of your rabbit excitedly hopping towards you, eager for some cuddles and playtime.

Owning a rabbit is not just about the laughter and joy they bring. It is also a journey of learning, patience, and responsibility. Rabbits are delicate creatures that require a safe, comfortable, and clean environment to live in. As a rabbit owner, you must ensure that your furry friend has a spacious and secure home, complete with soft bedding, nutritious food, and fresh water.

It's important to remember that rabbits love to chew, dig, and explore. To keep your rabbit entertained and happy, provide them with toys and activities that cater to their natural instincts. Cardboard boxes, tunnels, and chew toys can make excellent additions to your rabbit's play area, allowing them to expend their energy in a fun and safe manner.

Nutrition is a key aspect of rabbit care. Rabbits have sensitive digestive systems, and they require a balanced diet of hay, vegetables, and a small number of pellets to stay healthy. Treats should be given in moderation, as overfeeding can lead to obesity and other health issues. As a responsible rabbit owner, you must ensure that your rabbit receives the proper nutrition to maintain their health and happiness.

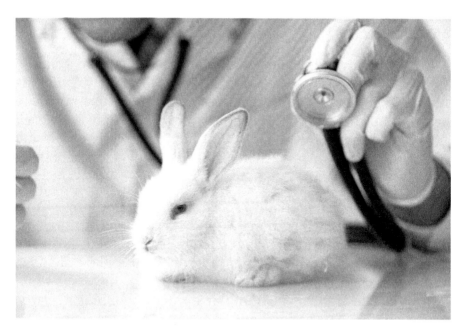

Just like humans need check-ups at the doctor, rabbits need regular check-ups with a veterinarian to ensure they're in tip-top shape. It's essential to find a veterinarian who specialises in rabbit care, as they will be best equipped to handle your rabbit's unique needs. Regular check-ups can help prevent illnesses and ensure that your rabbit receives the necessary vaccinations and treatments to stay healthy.

Rabbits are intelligent creatures that require mental stimulation and social interaction to thrive. Spending time with your rabbit, talking to them, and engaging them in play can help strengthen the bond between you and your furry friend. It's also essential to provide your rabbit with the opportunity to interact with other rabbits, as this will help them develop important social skills and prevent loneliness.

While owning a rabbit can be an incredibly rewarding experience, it's important to remember that they are a long-term commitment. Depending on the breed, rabbits can live between 3-12 years, and they require consistent care and attention throughout their lives. Before adopting a rabbit, make sure you're prepared for the responsibility of providing them with a loving and nurturing home for the entirety of their life.

Rabbits are the embodiment of joy, love, and friendship. They are creatures that touch our hearts with their gentle nature and boundless energy, teaching us the importance of kindness and compassion. But like all living beings, rabbits also require care, respect, and commitment. As a responsible rabbit owner, you must step up to the challenge and embrace the joys and responsibilities that come with sharing your life with a rabbit.

As you embark on this journey, remember that every hop and every cuddle is a testament to the love that you and your rabbit share. So, let the adventure begin, and together, you and your rabbit will create a world filled with happiness, laughter, and a bond that will last a lifetime.

Chapter 30 - Bunny Banter: FAQ's

Welcome, fellow bunny enthusiasts, to the chapter where curiosity meets knowledge, and questions leap into answers. In our rabbit-raising journey, it's natural to be brimming with queries, and we're here to unravel the mysteries! Let's hop into the bustling warren of rabbit wisdom with our FAQ session.

Why does my rabbit thump its foot?

Your bunny isn't just a fluffy friend but a skilled drummer too! That thumping sound you hear is their way of sending a rabbit SOS. They might be alerting their fellow bunnies – or their human friends – about a potential danger. So, if your rabbit starts playing their foot drum, it's time to ensure everything is safe and secure.

Can my rabbit swim?

Rabbits are miraculous creatures, but they're not natural Michael Phelpses. In fact, swimming can be stressful and even dangerous for them. While their furry coats are marvellous for cuddles, they're not designed to dry quickly, making hypothermia a risk. So, let's skip the swimming lessons and stick to dry land adventures.

Why does my rabbit chew everything?

Bunnies are like tiny furry woodchippers. Those chompers never stop growing, and chewing helps keep them in check. It's also a great way for rabbits to explore their world. So, if your bunny is turning your home into a chew toy, it's time to invest in some rabbit-safe toys and make sure all cables and dangerous items are out of reach.

Is it okay for my rabbit to eat grass from the lawn?

Yes, your rabbit can nibble on your lawn, turning your garden into a bunny buffet! But, ensure it's free from pesticides or any other chemicals. Also, remember, grass is not a substitute for hay, which should make up the bulk of their diet.

Why do my rabbit's eyes appear red in photos?

No, your rabbit hasn't been cast in a vampire movie. Rabbits, like many animals, have a layer in their eyes called the tapetum that helps them see in low light. This layer can reflect light back through the retina, causing the spooky red-eye effect in photos.

Why does my rabbit nudge me with its nose?

A rabbit nudge can be a gentle hello, a request for attention, or even a polite plea for you to move out of their way. It's their adorable way of communicating with you. Respond with gentle strokes and bunny-approved treats.

My rabbit flopped onto its side suddenly, is it okay?

Fear not, your bunny hasn't fainted. The sudden flop is a sign of a supremely content rabbit. It's their version of lounging on a hammock in the sunshine. It means they feel safe and comfortable, so give yourself a pat on the back for creating such a bunny-friendly environment.

Why does my rabbit grind its teeth?

Much like a purring cat, a gently teeth-grinding rabbit is a content bunny! This 'tooth purring' often happens when you're petting them just right. However, louder grinding could signal discomfort or pain, so if it's noticeable and frequent, a vet visit might be in order.

Why does my rabbit dig at the carpet?

Your living room carpet isn't a beach, but try telling that to a bunny! Rabbits are born diggers, and this behaviour is an echo of their wild instincts. To save your carpet, provide alternatives like digging boxes filled with safe, shreddable materials.

Can rabbits see colour?

While your rabbit might not appreciate a rainbow as we do, they're not colourblind. Rabbits can see some colours, primarily blues and greens. They can't see the full spectrum of colours as humans do, but their eyes are adapted to detect movement, perfect for spotting any sneaky predators!

How can I tell if my rabbit is too hot or too cold?

Rabbits are like Goldilocks; they prefer their temperature just right. If your bunny is too hot, you might notice them lying stretched out, breathing heavily, or even drooling. When too cold, they might hunch up and become less active. Always ensure they have a cool retreat in hot weather and a warm, draft-free area when it's chilly.

Why does my rabbit 'binky'?

Binky is the term for a rabbit's joyful leap and twist in mid-air, a delightful sight for any bunny parent. It's their way of saying, I'm happy, healthy, and full of energy! A binkying bunny is the epitome of rabbit joy.

Do rabbits dream?

As you watch your sleeping bunny twitching and moving its feet, you might wonder if they're dreaming. While we can't ask them directly, rabbits do go through similar sleep stages as humans, including REM sleep where dreaming occurs. So, it's possible they're chasing dreamland carrots!

Why is my rabbit's poop a different shape/size?

Rabbit poop can tell you a lot about their health. Regular rabbit droppings should be round and dry. If you notice a change, it might be related to their diet or hydration levels. However, if the change persists, it's time to consult a vet. Remember, rabbits also produce softer, nutrient-rich cecotropes which they reingest for extra nutrition.

Conclusion

As we hop to the end of this book, let's remember that the world of rabbits is as fascinating as it is varied. Their charming behaviours and endearing quirks are part of what makes them such amazing companions. But more than that, understanding these behaviours brings us closer to providing them with the best care possible, a responsibility every bunny parent should take to heart.

We've scratched the surface of some intriguing bunny questions in this chapter, but remember, every rabbit is unique! Your fluffy companion might have behaviours and habits all their own, and that's part of the joy of rabbit ownership - the continual discovery and understanding that unfolds.

Ultimately, the bond we share with our rabbits is a precious one, and it grows stronger with every bit of knowledge we gain about them. So, keep observing, learning, and loving your little hopper. Remember, you're their world, and to them, you're the biggest carrot in the patch.

Stay curious, bunny enthusiasts, and keep hopping along this incredible journey of companionship, responsibility, and love. Whether you're a veteran bunny parent or just starting, remember - in the world of rabbits, every day brings a new chance to learn and grow.

Keep your hearts open and your bunny cuddles plentiful. Here's to hopping happily ever after with your furry friends!

About the Author

Louisa Tarver is an enthusiastic author and avid explorer of the natural world. Her unwavering curiosity and deep love for nature are evident in every aspect of her writing, providing readers with a distinct perspective and enthralling insights. Among her previous works are "The Guinea Pig Care Guide" and "Do Insects Fart?"

Louisa's lifelong adoration for rabbits has shaped her understanding of these captivating creatures. From a tender age, their endearing personalities, intricate social dynamics, and adorable fluffy appearance captivated her attention. Hours spent observing and interacting with rabbits granted her valuable firsthand experience and profound insight into their unique needs and behaviours.

In addition to her published works, Louisa maintains the blog "Tarver's Guides," where readers can find additional information.

For anyone seeking to provide the best care for their furry companions, "Rabbits: The Ultimate Care Guide" is an essential read. Louisa Tarver's expertise and passion shine through, making this book a valuable resource for rabbit owners everywhere.

Also by Louisa Tarver

Hamsters: The Hamster Care Guide

Guinea Pigs: The Guinea Pig Care Guide

Do Insects Fart: 200 Creepy-Crawly Questions for Curious Kids

Would you Rather? Halloween: 201 Questions to Fright and Delight

Halloween: A History

Printed in Great Britain
by Amazon

32932738R00086